WITHDRAWN

Commentary on the <u>Lao Tzu</u>

Lao-Tzu.

COMMENTARY ON THE LAO TZU

by

Wang Pi

Translated by

Ariane Rump

In collaboration with

Wing-tsit Chan

MONOGRAPH NO. 6 OF THE

SOCIETY FOR ASIAN AND COMPARATIVE PHILOSOPHY

The University Press of Hawaii

1979

Library of Congress Cataloging in Publication Data

Lao-tzu.

    Commentary on the Lao Tzu.

    (Monograph of the Society for Asian and Comparative
Philosophy ; no. 6)

    Bibliography: p.

    I. Wang, Pi, 226-249. II. Rump, Ariane.
III. Chan, Wing-tsit, 1901- IV. Title. V. Series:
Society for Asian and Comparative Philosophy.
Monograph of the Society for Asian and Comparative
Philosophy ; no. 6.

BL1900.L26E5   1979b   299'.5148'2   79-11212

ISBN 0-8248-0677-8

TABLE OF CONTENTS

PREFACE

Professor Wing-tsit Chan made this book possible. It is to him that I am most deeply grateful; accordingly the effort applied to this work is an expression of thanks to him.

Lao Tzu, for centuries, has been and still is one of the most significant sources of inspiration and peace to the Eastern as well as the Western world. In this short classic, the laws fundamental to our lives are perceived out of deep lucidity. Generations upon generations are linked together in veneration of him.

Wang Pi (226-249) in his commentary on Lao Tzu, which is the oldest extant, goes beyond the boundaries of time and space, while penetrating in no lesser measure to the very core of human reality, and this he expresses among other terms in pen-t'i (substance) and li (principle). Wang Pi thus decisively anticipated the development of Neo-Confucian thinking.

The road given by my task was long. I owed the patience required to follow this path to C. G. Jung. A scholarship from the Board of Education and the University of Zurich made the realization possible. In particular I wish to thank Professors W. Heitler, G. Huber, R. P. Kramers, Verena Meyer, and A. Niederer.

For preliminary stages of the work I had the generous support of Mr. Ping-ming Hsiung of Paris, and Mr. Anthony Hu, Ph.D., of Taipei.

Mrs. Una Thomas has been of great assistance with the English translation. Dr. Henry Rosemont has kindly gone through the manuscript and has made many valuable improvements. The Bobbs-Merrill Co. has given permission to use Professor Wing-tsit Chan's English translation of the Lao Tzu text and Princeton University Press has also given permission to use Professor Chan's translation of Wang Pi's commentary. I wish to thank both publishers. Mrs. Olga Diethelm has repeatedly helped with the typing of the manuscript. Thanks are also due Dr. Eliot Deutsch, Chairman of the Monograph Series Committee, for bringing about this publication and for Mrs. Floris Sakamoto for preparing the manuscript for production. Most of all, I am grateful to the Society for Asian and Comparative Philosophy for including this translation in its Monograph Series.

I should like to express my gratitude to all of these persons, and to many others who have helped.

The present translation was completed in 1973, long before we learned of the publication of Professor Paul Lin's translation of Wang Pi's Commentary. I have been benefited by it, but only a few minor changes have been made as a result. Readers may be interested in Professor Chan's review of Lin's translation in Philosophy East and West, Vol. 29, No. 3 (July 1979).

Ariane Rump

INTRODUCTION

Of the several hundred extant commentaries on the Lao Tzu,[a] in China, Korea, and Japan, that by Wang Pi[b] (226-249) is outstanding in several respects. For one thing, it is the oldest. For another, it is the first and most philosophical. Third, it reversed the strong trend at his time of interpreting the Lao Tzu in religious and superstitious terms. Most important of all, it not only raised the understanding of Taoism to the metaphysical level but lifted Chinese philosophy itself to that level as well. It is not an exaggeration to say that Chinese metaphysics began with Wang's commentary on the Lao Tzu.

Wang's work does not merely consist of explanations of terms and a supply of data but is a deliberation on philosophical ideas. As such, the commentary goes beyond the Taoist classic. For example, in chapter 29, Lao Tzu talks about the sage discarding the extreme, the extravagant, and the excessive, but Wang Pi interprets it as the sage's understanding of the nature of Tzu-jan[c] (Self-so). In the same chapter, Lao Tzu speaks of the empire as "shen-ch'i,"[d] a spiritual thing, that is, something sacred, but Wang Pi looks upon shen as having neither form nor spatial restriction, in contrast to ch'i, which is a concrete thing formed by an integration of elements. In chapters 8, 21, 38, and 42, Wang goes beyond Lao Tzu and adds the concept of $\underline{wu}^e$ (non-being) to explain that while water is $\underline{yu}^f$ (being), Tao^g is nonbeing. Chapter 33 says that the wise person dies but does not really perish, but Wang talks about the everlasting Tao. In chapters 42 and 47, his departure from Lao Tzu is even more radical, for here he introduces the concept of $\underline{li}^h$ (principle). Similarly, in chapters 4, 6, and 38, whereas Lao Tzu speaks about the function of Tao and the universe, Wang goes a step further to discuss the substance which underlies their operation, thereby originating the concepts of substance and function ($\underline{t'i-yung}^i$).

The foregoing shows that Wang Pi was primarily interested in fundamental concepts. We shall now briefly discuss some of them.

First and foremost is, of course, the concept of Tao. As it is central in the Lao Tzu, so is it central in Wang's commentary. In this he follows Lao Tzu fairly closely. Tao is the greatest of all things that can be named (25). It is ahead of all things (62). It is everywhere and operates all around (34). It is infinite (59). All things and all values originate from it (34, 41, 51). It has neither form nor restriction, is not confined to any thing or form, and is really unnameable. These characteristics make Tao permanent and constant ($\underline{ch'ang}^j$) (1, 32). This aspect of constancy is perhaps more stressed than any other (16, 28, 32,

47); it is the Way for all times. The Tao of old can be used to master things of the present (14). Thus Tao is both in and above time, immanent and transcendent. It is the universal order and yet is above it.

Both the immanent and transcendental characters of Tao are implicit in the Lao Tzu, but Wang Pi brought in a new concept to explain how this was so. This is principle. The concept of principle is found in most ancient Chinese philosophical works. We encounter it in the Mo Tzu[k],[1] the Book of Mencius,[2] the Hsün Tzu[l],[3] the Chuang Tzu[m],[4] and the Han Fei Tzu[n],[5] among others. But its philosophical significance was not well established until the Wei[o] period (220-265), especially in the persons of Wang Pi and Kuo Hsiang[p] (d. 132), Kuo in his commentary on the Chuang Tzu and Wang in his commentary on the Book of Changes[6] and the Lao Tzu.[7]

The word li does not appear in the Lao Tzu at all but many times in Wang's commentary: in chapters 5, 36, 38, and 79, it is used in the primitive sense of "to manage" or "to put things in order"; in chapter 38, the term is also used to denote moral principles. Elsewhere, however, the meaning is definitely philosophical. It is by principle that all things can be understood (15). It is the "ultimate principle" embodied in Nature, which, if followed, will bring fortune, but if disobeyed, will bring misfortune (42). It is not only the principle of right and wrong but also the basis that combines all things into one because it possesses the quality of generality that governs all things (47). As Ch'ien Mu[q] has pointed out, instead of talking about Tao, Wang Pi talks about principle in a number of places.[8]

It should be noted that Wang's doctrine of principle is more developed in his commentary on the Book of Changes and in his essays on it.[9] Ch'ien Mu has listed nine instances where Wang Pi uses the term li to explain Change, including the use of such terms as t'ung-li[r] (general principle), pen-li[s] (fundamental principle), pi-jan chih-li[t] (necessary principle), so-i-jan chih-li[u] (principle by which things are), and chih-li[v] (ultimate principle).[10] In his essays, Wang Pi holds that Change is governed by principle; there is nothing that is not tied to it. It unites all things. It is one and universal. It transcends all phenomena. In his commentary on the Book of Changes, he sharply distinguishes principle, which is general, and facts, which are particular but he insists that the general principle can be discovered in any fact, so that the law of Change can be discovered in any event. As Ch'ien Mu has said, Wang practically anticipated all that the Sung (960-1279) Neo-Confucianists had to say about principle.[11]

In thus interpreting the process of Change on the basis of principle, Wang Pi effectively overthrew the tradition of Han (B.C. 206-220 A.D.) scholars who explained Change in terms of portents, strange phenomena, the interaction of man and Nature, and the influence of the Five Agents of Water, Fire, Wood, Metal, and Earth on human affairs. In doing so, he put Chinese scholarship on a rational and philosophical basis. What is more, he established a metaphysical system in China for the first time. So important is his commentary on the Book of Changes that the leading Neo-Confucianist, Ch'eng I[W] (1033-1107), recommended it among the first three commentaries for students to read, although he, as severe critic of Taoism as were all Neo-Confucianists, said that Wang Pi really did not understand Tao but merely explained it with the ideas of Lao Tzu and Chuang Tzu.[12] Still, it is true that he penetrated more deeply into the meanings of the Lao Tzu than he did the meanings of the Book of Changes.

One of the concepts in the Lao Tzu into which he penetrated most deeply is that of nonbeing. In saying that all being comes from nonbeing (1), that Tao has no shape, no name, and so on (14), and that things depend on nonbeing to function (11), Wang Pi is essentially repeating Lao Tzu. However, while Lao Tzu says that being and nonbeing produce each other, thus putting them on equal footing, Wang Pi considers nonbeing far more fundamental. According to him, only through nonbeing can Tao complete things and put them in order (23). Nonbeing is the mind (essence) of

Simplicity, which is Tao (32), as well as the mind of Heaven and Earth (38). To attain the constancy of Tao, it is necessary to achieve its vacuity and nothingness to the infinite and extreme degree (16). There can be no unity of things without it (42, 47). And only when there is nonbeing can being perform its function (38). Furthermore, Wang says, "Although it is valuable to have nonbeing as function, nevertheless there cannot be substance without nonbeing" (38). In other words, although nonbeing serves well for things to function, it must not be forgotten that it is substance. As such, nonbeing is original substance (pen-t'i^x).

This is clearly not the nonbeing that is opposed to being. In Lao Tzu the dichotomy still exists, Wang Pi thought Lao Tzu was not free from being but hoped for nonbeing and that was why he always "taught what he considered to be inadequate," that is, the nonbeing that was lacking in his philosophy.[13] For this reason, Wang Pi considered Confucius to be superior to Lao Tzu, because, according to him, Confucius "embodied nonbeing" whereas Lao Tzu could only embody being.[14] Since nonbeing is fundamental, it is the center of his philosophy. As T'ang Yung-t'ung^y has observed, Wang's metaphysics consists in regarding nonbeing as the original substance.[15]

Wang Pi often equates nonbeing with "roots" (pen^z) (38, 39, 52, 57, 58, 76) and "Mother" (1, 28,

39, 52, 59). "Mother" is Tao in its aspect of producing and completing things, whereas pen is Tao in its aspect of being fundamental. Pen as being fundamental is by no means absent in the Lao Tzu,[16] but Wang stresses it much more strongly, and, moreover, diametrically opposes it to mo[aa] or branches. Pen and mo, what is essential and what is subsidiary, or what is basic and what is secondary, are clearly distinguished. In fact, he was the first to treat pen-mo as a metaphysical question in Chinese history, although in its practical sense, the term is found in the Great Learning.[17] By the roots he means non-being, Tao, principle, the Mother, original substance, and by branches he means the world in operation. He says, "The Mother should not be discarded and the roots should not be lost . . . . If one discards one's Mother and uses her son, and if one discards the roots and goes towards the branches, . . . there will surely be trouble" (38). On the surface, Wang seems to be a pure transcendentalist looking upon the world of events as subordinate. But that is not the case. This is what he says: "Mother is the roots and son is the branches. One should find the roots in order to understand the branches" (52). Again, "Hold on to the Mother in order to preserve the son . . . . Honor the roots in order to promote the branches" (38). In short, he maintains that roots and branches are of equal value.

xv

This can best be seen in his concept of substance and function. The word t'i does not appear in the Lao Tzu, but in Wang's commentary it occupies a key position (4, 6, 23, 25, 38). According to him, it is the ultimate (6). This means that it is Mother, roots, and nonbeing all rolled in one.

His concept of substance and function is perhaps the most creative in his philosophy. The thirty-eighth chapter of the commentary may be said to be a treatise on it. It deals with the relationship between Tao as substance and te^{ab} (virtue, character) as function. As roots and branches go together, so substance and function must go hand in hand. "As nonbeing is its (virtue's) function," Wang says, "all things will be embraced . . . . Although Heaven and Earth are extensive, non-being is the mind. . . . Therefore if one destroys oneself and one's ego, then all people within the four seas will respect and will come to him from far and near" (38). In other words, with nonbeing as substance, all things will function well. At the same time, "Although it is valuable to have non-being as function, nevertheless there cannot be substance without non-being." That is to say, substance and function involve each other. In the ultimate sense, they are identical. This has become a general pattern in Chinese philosophy. As I have said in an earlier work:

This is the first time in the history
of Chinese thought that substance and
function are mentioned together. In the
Book of Changes, it is said that "the
state of absolute quiet and inactivity . . . .
when acted on, immediately penetrates all
things."[18] Neo-Confucianists interpreted
the two states as substance and function,
but they are so only by implication. The
concepts of substance and function definitely
originated with Wang Pi. They were to
become key concepts in Chinese Buddhism
and Neo-Confucianism.[19]

The correct way to function, whether in the
universe or in the human world, is to follow Tzu-jan,
which means Nature, being natural, self-so, and so on.
The term appears in the Lao Tzu five times but twenty-
four times in Wang's commentary, in almost one-third
of the eighty-one chapters.[20] He frequently uses such
terms as yin[ac] (to follow, in accordance with),[21]
jen[ad] (leave things alone),[22] and shun[ae] (to follow,
to obey).[23] Where Lao Tzu talks about concentrating
one's vital force (10), possessing no body (13),
traveling wisely (27), taking no action (37), or
having the greatest skill (45), Wang Pi has added
tzu-jan as the cause. The same explanation is offered
for the wise man not to talk (56), for serving Heaven
(59), for spiritual beings not to harm people (60),

for being able to do things without studying (64), and for the ruler to keep the people ignorant (65).

Elaborating on Lao Tzu's idea, Wang Pi says, "Heaven and Earth leave <u>Tzu-jan</u> alone. They do nothing and create nothing. The myriad things manage and order themselves . . . . If one discards oneself and leaves things alone, then everything will be in order" (5). Again, "If one acts according to <u>Tzu-jan</u> without creating or starting things, things will therefore reach their goal" (27). When things are left alone, they will all arise, have support, and be preserved (38).

To Wang Pi, however, <u>Tzu-jan</u> is not merely following Nature. It is, he says, "something that cannot be labeled and something ultimate" (25). What is this ultimate? There is no doubt that in Wang Pi's mind it is the roots, the original substance, or the Mother. In short, it is Tao in the highest sense. "The Tao of <u>Tzu-jan</u> is like a tree," he says. "The further we go to the branches, the further away are we from the roots" (22). With reference to the operation of the universe, to follow <u>Tzu-jan</u> means to follow principle (15). With reference to the ways of man and things, to follow <u>Tzu-jan</u> means to follow their nature (<u>hsing</u>^{af}). "The nature of the myriad things is <u>Tzu-jan</u>. It should be followed and not be interfered with" (29). Blindness, and so forth, results because one does not act in accordance with his nature and destiny but, on the contrary, injures his Tzu-jan (12). "Always follow the nature of things, he urges (27, 36, 41). When Tzu-jan prevails, all is well and nothing is wanting, for Tzu-jan is self-sufficient (20). Moreover, it has infinite potentiality." Heaven and Earth...leave things in the state of Tzu-jan...and they cannot be exhausted (5). It is like the standard of a circle. If it is followed, the number of circles that can be drawn is unlimited (25). For Tao itself, it does not oppose Tzu-jan and therefore it attains its nature (25).

The one who realizes Tzu-jan to the highest degree is the sage. "The sage understands Tzu-jan perfectly and knows the condition of all things. Therefore he goes along with them but takes no unnatural action. He is in harmony with them but does not impose anything on them....Things will then be contented with their nature" (29).

From the preceding, it is clear that Wang Pi has raised the philosophy of Lao Tzu to a higher level. In so doing, he inaugurated a new era in the history of Chinese philosophy and in several ways anticipated Neo-Confucian thought, especially in the concepts of substance and function and those of nature and principle.

Having surveyed Wang's philosophy, we may now proceed to give a brief account of his life and commentary.

Wang Pi (courtesy name, Fu-ssu[ag]) was born in 226 in Kao-p'ing[ah] county, Shan-yang[ai] Prefecture,[24] in Shantung Province. His grandfather, Wang K'ai[aj], fleeing from political turmoils and rebellions, went along with a clansman Wang Ts'an[ak] (177-217) to Ching-chou[al].[25] The governor of Ching-chou Province, Liu Piao[am] (144-208), had attracted more than a thousand outstanding men of literature and thought. At first, he wanted to give his daughter in marriage to Wang Ts'an, but finding him ugly and Wang K'ai handsome, took Wang K'ai instead as his son-in-law. K'ai had a son Yeh[an], who had two sons, Hsüan[ao] and Pi.

Ts'ai Yung[ap] (132-129), the famous scholar who, by imperial command, collected the texts of the Six Confucian Classics[26] and had them inscribed on stone in 175, possessed a library of about ten thousand books. At his old age, he gave the collection to Wang Ts'an. After Ts'an's death, his son was involved in a rebellion and was executed. The collection then came into the hands of Wang Yeh. Thus from his childhood, Wang Pi had access to perhaps the best library of the time.

There is no question that Wang Pi was a genius. He had a brilliant mind and loved to argue. As a teenager, he was fond of the Lao Tzu and the Chuang Tzu. When he was twenty, he went to visit his father's colleague P'ei Hui[aq] (fl. 230-249). At

that time, his father was a director of the grand
secretariat in the state of Wei[ar] at its capital
Loyang and P'ei Hui was a director of the department
of civil personnel. P'ei asked him why Confucius did
not talk about nonbeing whereas Lao Tzu did. Wang Pi
expressed the radical opinion that Lao Tzu was not
free from being (as opposed to nonbeing) and that
was why he always taught what he considered to be
inadequate.[27] At that time, Ho Yen[as] (190-249) was
minister of the department of civil personnel. He
always had many guests, including able talkers. He
presented his superb ideas to Wang Pi and asked if
the youngster could refute him. Refute he did! Then
he himself proceeded to deliberate, giving both
questions and answers and none could match him.[28]
Greatly impressed with him, Ho Yen declared, "One
may discuss with him the boundary between Heaven
and man."

In the middle of the Cheng-shih[at] period (240-
249), Ho Yen was considering Wang Pi for a director-
ship in the imperial chancellery when a position
became vacant. Instead, the appointment went to
Wang Li[au], recommended by Ho Yen's rival to Regent
Ts'ao Shuang[av] (d. 249), who actually controlled the
kingdom of Wei. As a result, Wang Pi was made a
departmental director. Soon after he assumed office,
he asked to see the regent alone without any atten-
dant around and for more than an hour talked about

philosophical principles and nothing else. Ts'ao
Shuang chided him for this.

His fame soared. He and Ho Yen became the
celebrated scholars of the Cheng-shih period.[29] Although Kuo Hsiang's commentary on the Chuang Tzu
was often mentioned together with Wang's on the Lao
Tzu, Kuo was regarded as inferior to Wang.[30] Wang's
discussions were considered as "the sound of the
Cheng-shih period" and "the sound of gold."[31] Before
Ho Yen finished his commentary on the Lao Tzu, he
went to see Wang Pi. As Wang Pi expounded on the
ideas of Lao Tzu, Ho Yen could not say anything except
"yes, yes." Thereupon he gave up his commentary on
the Lao Tzu and wrote the Treatise on Tao and Te
instead.[32]

Wang Pi's ability did not measure up to his
official responsibilities but he did not care. Being
good at music and at the game of throwing arrows into
a distant pot, he enjoyed social parties at which he
could demonstrate his skill. In literary composi-
tion, he was not Ho Yen's equal, but in exceptional
natural gifts he far surpassed Ho. Because of this,
he often snubbed others. Naturally, many did not
like him. He was at first friendly with Wang Li and
Hsün Jung[aw] (233-263), but because he lost the
position to the former, he hated him, and his friend-
ship with the latter did not last long either. In
249, when Ts'ai Shuang was killed in a power struggle,

Wang Pi was dismissed from office. In the fall of
that year, he encountered a pestilence and died
suddenly. He was twenty-four and was the youngest
Chinese philosopher to die at an early age. He had
no son but a daughter who was married to Chao Chi-
tzu.[ax] It was from this family that Chang Chan[ay]
(fl. 310) found six chapters of the Lieh Tzu[az] which
he eventually annotated.[33] Incidentally, Chang Chan's
mother was Wang Pi's first cousin.[34]

The present translation is based on the Ssu-pu
pei-yao[ba] (Essentials of the Four Libraries) edition,
a reproduction of the Chü-chen[bb] (Collected treasures)
edition of the Wu-ying[bc] Palace of 1775. It contains
an epilogue dated 1115 by Chao Yüeh-chih[bd] (1059-
1129) which says that the work was called Tao-te
ching[be] (Classic of the Way and virtue) but not
divided into two parts, that there were many mistakes,
and that he made a copy of it in October. There is
also an epilogue by Hsiung K'o[bf] (c. 1111-c. 1184).
He said that the Wang Pi commentary was very rare
and he found one only after a long search. After he
published it, he came upon Chao's version. Since it
was not divided into two parts or chapters, he thought
it was an old edition. He therefore copied it and, in
1170, published it. Following these two epilogues,
there is the portion on Wang Pi's commentary from the
Ching-tien shih-wen[bg] (Explanations of words in the
classics) by Lu Te-ming[bh] (556-627).

The commentary has gone through a number of changes in title, format, and wording. It is called Lao Tzu tao-te ching[bi] (annotated by Wang Pi) in the Sui shu[bj] (History of the Sui dynasty, 581-618),[35] the Yüan-yen hsin-chi tao-te[bk] (New record of profound words on the Way and its virtue) in the Chiu T'ang shu[bl] (History of T'ang dynasty, 618-907),[36] the Hsin-chi yüan-yen tao-te in the Hsin T'ang shu[bm] (New history of the T'ang Dynasty),[37] and Lao Tzu chu[bn] (Commentary on the Lao Tzu) in the Sung shih[bo] (History of the Sung dynasty).[38] According to Takeuchi[bp], the use of the terms "new record" and "profound words" was common in the T'ang Dynasty for Taoist works, especially in the Lao Tzu and the Chuang Tzu.[39] As already noted, the work became rare in the Sung period. In the middle of the Wan-li[bq] period (1573-1619) of the Ming dynasty (1368-1644), Chang Chih-hsiang[br] (1496-1577) published the Chao version of 1115. It has become the standard edition and has formed the basis for other editions in both China and Japan. It was collated in 1782 according to the Yung-lo ta-tien[bs] (Great library of the Yung-lo period, 1403-1428) edition. The Yung-lo edition, however, contains only the first part of the Wang Pi commentary. Modern collations have been made by T'ao Hung ch'ing[bt] (1860-1918), Liu Kuo-chün[bu], Hatano[bv], and Yen-ling Feng.[bw] Hatano's study is virtually exhaustive. Tao's collation is essential and Yen has improved upon it. Liu's collation is based on only two commentaries.

A number of points concerning the Wang Pi commentary has been debated by scholars for years. One is whether the commentary is indeed the oldest extant commentary on the Lao Tzu. The earliest commentary on some Lao Tzu passages is, of course, that in the Han Fei Tzu. The bibliography section of the Han shu[bx] (History of the Former Han dynasty, B.C. 206-8 A.D.) lists three commentaries but these have disappeared.[40] Later bibliographies list ten before Wang and five of Wang's time.[41] All of them have been lost.

The oldest extant commentary on the Lao Tzu text as such is probably the "Hsiang-erh[by]" commentary. Only Part One of that commentary has survived. Neither its date nor its author is known, though some have suggested that Chang Ling[bz] (fl. 156), the founder of the Taoist religion, was the author.[42] Of the seven-hundred-odd Chinese commentaries and about two hundred and fifty Japanese commentaries on the Lao Tzu written in the last sixteen hundred years, about four hundred are still extant. Beyond any dispute, the oldest extant complete commentaries are those by Wang Pi and Ho-shang Kung[ca] (Old man up the river).

The two commentaries have also been the most popular. Yen Ling-fen has listed thirty-four

editions of the Wang Pi commentary and thirty-three
of the Ho-shang Kung commentary.[43] The former is
strictly philosophical and therefore has appealed to
intellectuals while the latter is a religious interpretation and therefore has appealed to devout
Taoist followers. Ho-shang Kung is supposed to
have lived in the second century B.C. If he ever
lived and ever wrote a commentary, that must have
disappeared very early. The present Ho-shang Kung
commentary, in the opinion of most scholars, came
after the Wang Pi commentary. Eduard Erkes, who has
translated the Ho-shang Kung commentary into English,
strongly maintained that it existed before the
second century,[44] and offered three arguments for
the early dating. The first is that Kao Yu[cb] (fl. 205)
interpreted the word hsüan[cc] in his commentary on
the Huai-nan Tzu[cd] as heaven.[45] Since the term
comes from the Lao Tzu and Ho-shang Kung interpreted
it as heaven, Erkes thought that Kao Yu must have
known about the Ho-shang Kung commentary. Erkes
does not explain why Ho-shang Kung could not have
borrowed from Kao Yu. His second argument is that
Mou Tzu[ce] mentions that the Classic of Te has thirty-
seven chapters,[46] which is the arrangement of the
Ho-shang Kung commentary. But whether Mou Tzu
existed in the first or third century is by no means
a settled question. Erkes offers the preface to the
commentary ascribed to Ko Hsüan[cf] (fl. 210) as his
third argument, but the preface contains too many

fantastic accounts and anachronisms to be reliable.[47]
According to Ma Hsü-lun[cg], the first mention of the
Ho-shang Kung commentary did not take place until
the fourth century, and its first listing in a
catalogue was in the Liang period (502-527).[48]
Remarking on the two commentaries, Takeuchi, noting
that where the Wang Pi commentary has archaic words
and difficult expressions the Ho-shang Kung commentary has standard words and plain expressions, said
that obviously the latter is a later product.[49]
These two scholars are not alone in this majority
opinion.

Another question is the format of the Wang Pi
commentary. Both Chao Yüeh-chih and Hsiung K'o
thought that the commentary was not divided into
parts or chapters. Editors of the Ssu-k'u ch'üan-
shu tsung-mu t'i-yao[ch] (Essentials of the complete
catalogue of the Four Libraries) perpetuated this
opinion and explained the fact that the Ching-tien
shih-wen is actually divided into the Tao-ching[ci]
(Classic of the Way) and Te-ching[cj] (Classic of
virtue) simply by saying that the arrangement is a
later imposition.[50] But as many scholars have
pointed out, the work has been divided into Tao-
ching and Te-ching since Han times.[51] As Wang
Chung-min[ck] has observed, Hsiung K'o was amazed at
the absence of division into parts or chapters in
the Chao Yüeh-chih edition only after he had
published his. This clearly shows that his earlier

version was divided into parts and chapters.[52]

The strongest proof that the original edition of the Wang Pi commentary had two parts and many chapters is a fact known to many scholars, namely, that Wang Pi himself refers to a "Part 2" in chapter 20 and "a later chapter" in chapters 23 and 28. It is not unusual for the same work to appear in different formats. In this case, whether it is called Lao Tzu chu or Tao-te ching chu, whether divided into parts and chapters, and whether in one volume (chuan^{cl}) or in two volumes (each part being a chuan) was of no real consequence. In its standard form, it has been divided into two parts from Han times and has been called the Lao Tzu chu, Tao-te ching chu, or Lao Tzu tao-te ching chu. The most radical departure is the edition in the Tao-tsang^{cm} (Taoist canon). It has four chapters. According to a Japanese writer, the reason for this is to conform with the fourfold division of the canon.[53]

Still another question is whether the Lao Tzu wei-chih lüeh-li^{cn} (Brief presentation of the subtle ideas of Lao Tzu) was written by Wang Pi. In his biography of Wang Pi, Ho Shao^{co} (236-301) said that "in annotating the Lao Tzu, Wang Pi presented the essential ideas to achieve a rational system; he wrote the Tao-lüeh lun^{cp} (Brief discussion on Tao)."[54] Up to the Sung times, works bearing the titles of Lao Tzu lüeh-lun^{cq} (Brief discussion on the Lao Tzu), Lao Tzu chih li-lüeh[cr] (Brief presentation of the ideas of the Lao Tzu), Lao Tzu chih-lüeh[cs] (Essential ideas of Lao Tzu), and Tao-te lüeh-kuei[ct] (Brief conclusions on the Way and virtue), scholars like Wong Chung-min, N. Z. Zia[cu], and Yen Ling-fen agree, are the same work.[55] Most likely the titles were derived from Ho Shao's Tao lüeh-lun, which has disappeared long ago. However, Zia has suggested that while most of the Wang Pi commentary is in concise, classical style, passages in chapters 4 and 38 are not explanations but interpretations and the style is that of a short essay. Zia thought these passages may have come from the Lao Tzu chih-kuei.[56] This is an interesting suggestion, but we need concrete proofs.

In the Tao-tsang there is the Lao Tzu wei-chih lüeh-lun.[57] In 1946, Yen Ling-fen published it and vigorously maintains that it is by Wang Pi. He compares Wang Pi's commentary and the Lao Tzu wei-chih lüeh-li and points out that first, there are twelve instances of similar passages, and, second, three instances of similar literary construction and two instances of similar quotations from the Book of Change.[58] Mou Tsung-san[cv] has hailed this discovery as a great contribution.[59]

However, I have found Yen's identification difficult to accept. Surely there is a great deal of similarity between the Lao Tzu wei-chih lüeh-li and the Wang Pi commentary. Nevertheless, the former seems to be a repetition or an elaboration. In addition, many basic ideas of the commentary are not found in the Lao Tzu wei-chih lüeh-li, such as those of constancy, honoring the roots, principle, the inadequacy of names, and so forth. The fundamental concepts of the commentary, particularly those of substance and function, nonbeing, oneness, following Tao and leaving things alone (yin, yen, shun), and Tzu-jan, are either totally absent or hardly present in the Lüeh-li. On the other hand, the literary style is simple and plain and does not have the elegance or the conciseness of the commentary. The work has sets of five such as the Five Grains, the Five Things, and the Five Notes, as well as the names of the Confucian, Moist^{cw}, and Legalist schools, which do not appear in the commentary. It seems to me that the work in question was written on the basis of the commentary by someone who did not quite understand Wang Pi's new philosophical ideas, especially the cardinal concepts of nonbeing, Tzu-jan, and substance and function.

In the course of her work on the Book of Changes,[60] Dr. Ariane Rump became interested in Wang Pi's commentaries. She made a translation of the commentary on the Lao Tzu. I have suggested changes, added most of the footnotes, and prepared the bibliography. It is hoped that this English translation will contribute to the understanding of the <u>Lao Tzu</u> as a work of philosophy, will encourage Western scholars to pay more attention to this third-century metaphysician who is still largely unknown to the West, and throw some light on the importance of third-century thought in the development of Chinese philosophy.

Wing-tsit Chan[cx]

NOTES

1. Mo Tzu, (by Mo Ti[cy], 468-376 B.C.?),
chapter 3, Ssu-pu ts'ung-k'an[cz] (Four Libraries
series) ed. 1:6b, 9:18a, 9:19b.

2. Book of Mencius, 5A:1, 6A:7.

3. Hsün Tzu (by Hsün Ch'ing[da], 313-238 B.C.?),
passim.

4. Chuang Tzu (by Chuang Chou[db], 369-268
B.C.?), passim.

5. Han Fei Tzu (by Han Fei, d. 233 B.C.), Ssu-
pu ts'ung-k'an ed., especially 6:7a.

6. In the Thirteen Classics.

7. For a story of the development of the concept of li in Chinese philosophy, see my "The Evolution of the Neo-Confucian Concept Li as Principle,"
in Tsing Hua[dc] Journal of Chinese Studies, n. s. 4,
no. 2 (February 1964), pp. 123-138; reprinted in Neo-
Confucianism, Etc.; Essays by Wing-tsit Chan (Hanover, N.H.: Oriental Society, 1969), pp. 45-87.

8. "Wang Pi Kuo Hsiang chu I Lao Chuang yung
li-tzu t'iao-lu[dd]" (Cases of the use of the term li
in Wang Pi's and Kuo Hsiang's commentaries on the
Book of Changes, the Lao Tzu, and the Chuang Tzu),
Hsin-Ya hsüeh-pao[de] (New Asia journal), 1, no. 1
(April 1955), p. 137.

9. The Chou-i lüeh-li[df] (Simple exemplification
of the principles of the Book of Changes) in the Han-
Wei ts'ung-shu[dg] (Collection of works of the Han and
Wei dynasties). For an English translation of part

1, the most important chapter, see my A Source Book
in Chinese Philosophy, pp. 318-319, and for an
English translation of part 4 from the German, see
Hellmut Wilhelm, Die Wandlung (Peking, Vetch, 1944),
pp. 129-132; also in his Change, Eight Lectures on
the I ching,[dh] trans. by Carey F. Baynes (New York:
Pantheon, 1960), pp. 87-88.

10. Op. cit. (see note 8), pp. 135-137.

11. Ibid.

12. I-shu[di] (Surviving works), in the Erh-Ch'eng
ch'üan-shu[dj] (Complete works of the two Ch'engs),
Ssu-pu pei-yao ed., 19:1b, 1:6a.

13. Liu I-ch'ing[dk] (403-444), Shih-shuo hsin-
yü,[dl] chapter 4, section 8; English translation by
Richard B. Mather, Shih-shuo hsin-yü, A New Account
of Tales of the World (Minneapolis, Minnesota:
University of Minnesota Press, 1966), p. 96.

14. Ibid.

15. Wei-Chin hsüan-hsüeh lun-kao[dm] (Draft treatise on Wei-Chin [220-420] metaphysics), p. 50.

16. Lao Tzu, chapters 26, 39.

17. The text and chapter 10.

18. "Appended Remarks", Part I, chapter 10.

19. See my A Source Book in Chinese Philosophy,
p. 323.

20. Lao Tzu, chapters 17, 23, 25, 51, 64; Wang's
commentary, 2, 5, 10, 13, 15, 17, 20, 22, 23, 25, 27,
28, 29, 37, 41, 42, 45, 49, 56, 59, 60, 64, 65, 77.

21. Chapters 2, 10, 27, 29, 36, 41, 45, 47, 49,

51, 56.

22. Chapters 5, 10, 38, 81.

23. Chapters 12, 27, 37, 42, 65, 81. Also ts'ung[dn] (to follow) in chapter 21.

24. Present Chin-hsiang[do] county.

25. Its provincial seat was the present Hsiang-yang[dp] county, Hupei province.

26. Book of Odes, Book of History, Book of Changes, Book of Rites, Spring and Autumn Annals, and Book of Music.

27. Shih-shuo hsin-yü (see note 13), chapter 4, section 8; Mather's translation, p. 96.

28. Ibid., chapter 4, section 6; Mather, p. 95.

29. Ibid., chapter 4, section 85, 94; Mather, pp. 137, 140.

30. Ibid., chapter 4, section 17; Mather, p. 100.

31. Ibid., chapter 8, section 51; Mather, p. 226.

32. Ibid., chapter 4, section 10; Mather p. 97.

33. Chang Chan's preface to the Lieh Tzu.

34. Ch'ü Yung[dq] (fl. 1840), T'ieh-ch'in T'ung-chien Lou mu-lu[dr] (Catalogue of the T'ieh-ch'in T'ung-chien Hall), chapter 18, Taoist school section, under Ch'ung-hsü chih-te chen-ching[ds] (Pure classic of the perfect virtue of simplicity and vacuity). Most of this biographical material has been taken from the standard biography of Wang Pi by Ho Shao

quoted by P'ei fung-chih[dt] (372-451) as a note to the biography of Chung Hui[du] (225-264) in the Wei chih[dv] (History of the state of Wei), chapter 28, and the "Pi pieh-chuan[dw]" (Separate biography of Wang Pi) quoted in the note to the Shih-shuo hsin-yü, chapter 4, section 4 (Mather, p. 95. See note 13).

35. Chapter 34, section on the Taoist school.

36. Chapter 47, section on the Taoist school.

37. Chapter 59, section on the Taoist school.

38. Chapter 205, section on the Taoist school.

39. Rōshi genshi[dx] (Origins of the Lao Tzu), pp. 62-64.

40. By Lin[dy], Fu[dz], and Hsü[ea],

41. The ten are: Lin, Fu, Hsü, Liu Hsiang[eb] (77-6 B.C.), Yen Tsun[ec] (fl. 53-24 B.C.), Mu-ch'iu Wang-chih[ed] (c. 20 B.C.-22 A.D.), Ma Jung[ee] (79-166), Sung Chung[ef] (fl. 191-219), Yü Fan[eg] (164-233), and Chang I[eh] (fl. 221-239). The five are: Hsün Jung, Fan Wang[ei] (d. 264), Tung Yü[ej] (fl. 227-264), Chung Hui, and Ho Yen.

42. For a comprehensive account of the Hsiang-erh commentary, see Jao Tsung-i[ek], Lao Tzu hsiang-erh chu chiao-chien[el] (The "hsiang-erh" commentary on the Lao Tzu collated and commented on).

43. Chung-wai Lao Tzu chu-shu mu-lu[em] (Bibliography on the Lao Tzu in Chinese and foreign languages), pp. 373-377. See also Wang Chung-min, Lao Tzu k'ao[en] (Inquiry on the Lao Tzu), p. 78,

where he lists fourteen Chinese editions and two
Japanese editions (1770 and 1732).

44. Ho-shang Kung's Commentary on the Lao-tse.

45. Huai-nan Tzu[eo] (by Liu An[ep], 179-122 B.C.),
chapter 16, Ssu-pu pei-yao[eq] ed. (Essentials of the
Four Libraries), 16:6a.

46. Seng-yu[er] (445-518), comp., Hung-ming chi[es]
(Essays elucidating the doctrine), Ssu-pu pei-yao
ed., 1:12b.

47. Erkes, op. cit. (see note 44), pp. 10, 11.
See my The Way of Lao Tzu, pp. 78-81 for a discussion
on this question.

48. Lao Tzu chiao-ku[et] (Lao Tzu collated and
explained), pp. 2-3.

49. Rōshi genshi, p. 86.

50. (Shanghai, Commercial Press, 1933 edition),
p. 3033.

51. Hatano Tarō, Lao Tzu Wang chu chiao-cheng[eu]
(Wang Pi's Commentary on the Lao Tzu collated),
Part III, pp. 189-190, 192-193, 200, 203.

52. Wang Chung-min, op. cit. (see note 43),
p. 86.

53. Shimada Kan[ev], Ku-wen chiu-shu k'ao[ew]
(Inquiry on old works in the ancient script),
chapter 1, quoted in Hatano, Part III, p. 197.

54. See note 34, herein.

55. Yen Ling-fen, Lao Tzu wei-chih lüeh-li,
p. 5; Wang Chung-min. Lao Tzu k'ao, pp. 87-88; Zia
(see note 56), vol. 2, p. 621.

56. "Hsien-ts'un Tao-te ching chu-shih shu-mu k'ao-lüeh"[ex] (Brief inquiry on annotations and commentaries on the Classic of the Way and Virtue), Nan-hua Hsiao-chu Shan-fang wen-chi[ey] (Collected works of the Nan-hua Hsiao-chu Shan-fang), vol. 2 p. 655.

57. Cheng-i[ez] section, Ku[fa], Part I, no. 1245.

58. Lao Tzu wei-chih lüeh-li, pp. 6-15.

59. Ts'ai-hsing yü hsüan-li[fb] (Capacity, nature, and metaphysics), p. 137.

60. Die Verwundung des Hellen als Aspekt des Bösem im I ching (Cham, Switzerland: Gut-Druck AG, 1967).

CHAPTER 1

The Tao that can be told of is not the eternal Tao;

The name that can be named is not the eternal name.

The Tao that can be told of and the name that
can be named point to a particular affair and
construct a form but not their eternal aspect.

Therefore they cannot be told of or named.

The Nameless is the origin of Heaven and Earth;

The Named is the mother of all things.[1]

All being originated from nonbeing. The time
before physical forms and names appeared was
the beginning of the myriad things. After
forms and names appear, "Tao (the Way) develops
them, nourishes them, provides their formal
shape and completes their formal substance,"[2]
that is, becomes (or is) their Mother. This
means that Tao produces and completes things
with the formless and nameless. Thus they are
produced and completed[3] but do not know why.

Indeed it is the mystery of mysteries.[4]

Therefore let there always be no desire,[5] so we may
see their subtlety.[6]

Subtlety is the ultimate of minuteness.
The myriad things originate in subtlety
and afterward complete themselves. They
originate in nonbeing and afterward are
born. Therefore if we are always without

desire and empty,[7] we may see the subtlety of
these beginnings.

And let us always have desires, so we may see the
outcome.

Outcome means to come to an end. In general,
if being is to be useful, it has to function
through nonbeing.[8] Where a desire has roots,
these must be[9] in accord with Tao before they
come into realization. Thus if we always have
desire, we can observe the outcome of things
to the very end.

The two are the same,

But after they are produced, they have different
names.

They both may be called mystery.[10]

Mystery and more mystery.

The door of all subtleties![11]

"Both" means beginning and Mother. "The
same" and "produced" mean that together
they are produced from mystery. Having
different names, what applies to them cannot
be the same. At the start we call them
beginning and at the end we call them Mother.
Mystery is effacement, the silent, and nonbeing,
from which originate beginning and Mother.
Since we cannot name them, we cannot say they
both may be called mystery. But here they
are called mystery because there is no way out
but to call them so. If we call them so, then

we cannot say for sure that there is only one thing that is mysterious. That being the case[12] names fall far short of the truth. Hence it is said, "Mystery and more mystery"! All subtleties are produced from the same source and therefore it is said, "The door of all subtleties."

NOTES

1. Chan's note (The Way of Lao Tzu, p. 98, note 2): It is possible to punctuate wu-ming[a] (nameless) and yu-ming[b] (named) to mean "nonbeing is the name of" and "being is the name of", respectively. This is the reading by Duyvendak. Duyvendak refers to Ma Hsü-lun as authority; indeed, he depends chiefly on Ma. Ma did punctuate in this way in 1924 but in the revised edition of his book (1956), he has discarded the punctuation and has reverted to the generally accepted way as we have it. Wu-ming and yu-ming are key terms in the Lao Tzu, and are found also in chapters 32, 37, and 41.

2. Quoting Lao Tzu, ch. 51. According to Hatano Tarō, Lao Tzu Wang Chu Chiao Cheng (Wang Pi's commentary on the Lao Tzu corrected) (hereafter referred to as Hatano), I, p. 38, several Japanese commentators, referring to the Ch'u-hsüeh chi[c] (Records of initial learning), quoted Wang Pi's commentary on chapter 51 as saying "T'ing wei p'in ch'i hsing, tu wei ch'eng ch'i chih[d]." However, this is not found in the present Wang Pi commentary.

Arthur Waley, The Way and Its Power, p. 205, trans-
lates tu chih[e] in chapter 51 as "brewed for them,"
and says in the footnote the word tu means decoction,
whether nutritive, medical, or (as always in modern
Chinese) poisonous. The implication of decoction
may be right, as Tao in the end inevitably decocts
every being to its formal or its original substance.

3. I-shih i-ch'eng[f] (produces and completes)
also appears in chapter 21 of Wang Pi's commentary.
As Lao Ssu-kuang has pointed out in his Chung-kuo
che-hsüeh shih (History of Chinese philosophy)
(Shanghai: Commercial Press, 1931), p. 171, Fung
Yu-lan (Chung-kuo che-hsüeh shih, p. 608, not
translated by Derk Bodde in the History of Chinese
Philosophy) mispunctuated the sentence to read,
"Things are produced. Completed but do not...."

4. This paragraph has been adapted from Chan's
translation in his A Source Book in Chinese
Philosophy, p. 321. All quotations from the Source
Book are reprinted by permission of Princeton
University Press.

5. Chan's rendering: "Therefore let there
always be non-being so we may see their subtlety.
And let there always be being so we may see their
outcome." He has provided a long footnote (p. 99,
note 5) to explain his translation. The rendering
here is necessary to conform to Wang Pi's
understanding.

6. Chan's own note: (p. 99, note 4): This translation of miao[g] as "subtlety" rather than "mystery" is according to Wang Pi.

7. Hatano (I, p. 40) suggests that the words k'ung-hsü[h] (empty) are later additions. Hatano says two texts have added ch'i-huai[i] (its heart) under k'ung-hsü in order to make better sense, but he thinks k'ung-hsü is superfluous.

8. Wang Pi's expression i wu wei yung[j] (use nonbeing as function) also appears in Wang Pi chapters 11 and 40.

9. Shih[k] (to go to) is here understood as ho[l] (to accord).

10. Chan's original translation, "deep and profound." He noted (p. 100, note 8): The word hsüan[m] (deep and profound) has a very wide range of meanings; it means "dark," "abstruse," "deep," "profound," "secret," and so forth. In Taoist religion the aspect of mystery should be stressed, but in Taoist philosophy the profound or metaphysical aspect is paramount. The word simply has to be understood in its context.

11. Chan's own note (p. 100, note 9): Professor Boodberg has written an extremely provocative article on the translation of this chapter ("Philosophical Notes on Chapter One of Lao Tzu," Harvard Journal of Asiatic Studies, 20 [1957]: 598-618). He says that

"philologist should protest with the utmost vigor the common translation of Chinese yu and wu as 'Being' and 'Non-being' respectively....these two Chinese terms, even in Taoist environment, remained securely within the semantic and philosophical category of habit of possession, being both essentially transitive verbs, 'to have (something)' and 'not to have (something,' with objects following them in the normal course of grammatical and philosophical events" (p. 607). Evidently he overlooks the fact that in the Lao Tzu (chapters 2, 40, and so on), and in many places in the Chuang Tzu[n] (by Chuang Chou[o], 369-268 B.C.?), (especially chapters 2, 6, 12, 1:33b-34a, 3:15a, 5:9a...., Ssu-pu ts'ung-k'an[p] (Four Libraries series) ed., to mention only a few instances, yu[q] and wu[r] are not transitive verbs and do not mean "having" or "not having" anything.

12. The meaning of the corrupted text here is unclear.

CHAPTER 2

When the people of the world all know beauty as
   beauty,
There arises the recognition of ugliness.
When they all know the good as good,
There arises the recognition of evil.
Therefore: Being and nonbeing produce each other;
Difficult and easy complete each other;
Long and short contrast[1] each other;
High and low distinguish each other;
Sound and voice harmonize each other;
Front and behind accompany each other.

   The beautiful is what the human heart
   increasingly enjoys,[2] and ugliness is what
   the human heart hates and dislikes. Beauty
   and ugliness are comparable to joy and anger.
   Good and evil are comparable to right and
   wrong. Joy and anger have a common root.
   Right and wrong belong to the same family.[3]
   Therefore they should not be presented
   onesidedly. All these six are names and
   articles[4] that show Nature (Tzu-jan[a], self-so)
   should not be presented onesidedly.
Therefore the sage manages affairs without action.
   Nature herself suffices; he who acts
   (artificially) will meet with defeat.
And spreads doctrines without words.
All things arise, and he does not turn away from them.

He produces them but does not take possession of
them.

He acts but does not rely on his own ability.

Wisdom itself is complete; he who acts[5]
(artificially) is false.

He accomplishes his task but does not claim credit
for it.

(The sage) functions by following things.[6]

Success comes from them. Therefore (the
sage) claims no credit.

It is precisely because he does not claim credit that
his accomplishment remains with him.

If success lies in oneself, the accomplishment
will not last.

NOTES

1. Chan's note (p. 102, note 1): The Wang
Pi text has chiao[b] (to contrast) instead of hsing[c]
(to contrast). Evidently Waley (p. 257) has followed Wang Pi, but the Ho-shang Kung and, according
to Chiang Hsi-ch'ang, forty-six other texts, have
hsing. As Pi Yüan has pointed out, the word chiao
is not found in ancient books, and, according to
Ma Hsü-lun, whenever the long and the short are
contrasted in ancient literature, the word hsing
is used. Above all, chiao does not rhyme in the

verse but <u>hsing</u> does. Although both words mean the same, the Chinese character should be <u>hsing</u>.

2. According to Hatano, I, p. 45, the <u>Ku-i ts'ung-shu</u>[d] edition (Ancient and missing texts series) has <u>yüeh-chin</u>[e] (joy or music increases) instead of <u>chin-yüeh</u> (increasingly enjoys), obviously a mistake in reversing the order of the two words.

3. Compare Wang Pi, chapter 18.

4. <u>Ming-shu</u>[f] (clear number) is the same as <u>ming-shu</u> (name and articles) which define and clarify the names and reality of things.

5. According to a Japanese commentator, since this comment seems to be on "spreading doctrines without words," just as the preceding comment is on "manages affairs without action," perhaps the word <u>wei</u>[g] (to act) here should be amended to read <u>yen</u>[h] (to speak). See Hatano, I, p. 49.

6. <u>Yin</u>[i] (to follow [Nature] is a basic concept in Wang Pi. It is to appear again and again (chapters 27, 36, 41, 45, 49, 51, 56).

CHAPTER 3

Do not exalt the worthy, so that the people shall
   not compete.

Do not value rare treasures, so that the people
   shall not steal.

Do not display objects of desire, so that the
   people's[1] hearts shall not be disturbed.

      To be worthy means to be capable. To
exalt is to praise, and to value is to
glorify. Ability alone should be applied
to the task; what is the use of praising
(the worthy)? Utility alone should be
put into operation; what is the use of
valuing (rare treasures)? To exalt the
worthy and to make them famous is to
cause their fame to exceed their ability.
They will then act and always compete[2]
to try to overcome[3] one another.[4] When
goods are valued beyond their usefulness
the avaricious fight for their own benefit;
they break through or climb over walls[5]
and ransack trunks[6] at the risk of their
lives. (Thus) if we do not display objects
of desire, then the hearts will not be
disturbed.

Therefore in the government of the sage,

He keeps their hearts vacuous,[7]

Fills their bellies,

The heart harbors wisdom and the belly harbors
food. Vacuity means wisdom and to be full
means to be without cunning.

Weakens their ambitions,

And strengthens their bones,

Bones means to act without cunning. Ambition
means to create activities so as to disturb
(oneself). When the heart is vacuous, ambition
becomes weak.

He always causes his people to be without knowledge
(cunning) or desire,

This means to maintain their integrity (truth,
realness).

And the crafty to be afraid to act.

Craftiness means to act cunningly.

By acting without action, all things will be in
order.

NOTES

1. Chan's note (p. 104, note 4): This word appears in the Wang Pi text but does not appear in the Ho-shang Kung and forty-seven other texts. Its presence is necessary to maintain the parallelism of the three sentences.

2. According to T'ao Hung-ch'ing, the word chiao[a] (to compete) should be repeated, to read wei erh ch'ang-chiao, chiao neng hsiang-she[b] and to make the last sentence contain four characters. It would then read: They will then act and always compete; they will compete to try to overcome one another.

3. T'ao takes hsiang-she[c] to mean hsiang-sheng[d] (to overcome one another).

4. The Tao-te chen-ching chi-chu (Collected commentaries of the Classic of the Way and Virtue) version has yung kuo ch'i jen, hsia-pen erh ching, hsiao-neng hsiang-she[e] (Because their fame exceeds their ability, they will rush to compete and to exert their ability to overcome one another), instead of yung kuo ch'i jen, wei erh ch'ang-chiao, neng hsiang-she[f] (Because their fame exceeds their ability, they will then act and always compete to try to overcome one another).

5. The expression ch'uan-yü[g] (to break through or climb over walls) comes from the Analects, 17:12.

6. The expression t'an-ch'ieh[h] (to ransack trunks) comes from Chuang Tzu, chapter 10 (4:1ba).

7. Chan's note (p. 104, note 5): Hsü[i] (vacuous) is a Taoist term. It is not to be taken in its literal sense of being empty and is not to be equated with the Buddhist k'ung[j], which means emptiness or freedom from specific characteristics. Rather, as a description of a state of mind, it means absolute peacefulness and purity of mind, freedom from worry and selfish desires, not to be disturbed by incoming impressions or to allow what is already in the mind to disturb what is coming into the mind. As a feature of reality, it means a profound and deep continuum in which there is no obstruction.

CHAPTER 4

Tao is empty (like a bowl).

It may be used but its capacity is never exhausted.

It is bottomless, perhaps the ancestor of all things.

It blunts its sharpness,

It unties its tangles,

It softens its light.

It becomes one with the dusty world.

Deep and still, it appears to exist forever.

I do not know whose son it is.

It seems[1] to have existed before the Lord.

He who holds on to the capacity of a family
cannot perfect that family. He who holds
on to the capacity of a country cannot perfect
that country. When you exhaust your strength
to lift that which is heavy, you cannot perform
that function (yung[a], use). Truly, even if
one knows how to bring order into the myriad
things but does not do it through the Tao of
the two modes,[2] then one cannot bring them to
completion. Although the Earth is physical
body and soul, if it does not follow Heaven,
it cannot preserve its tranquility. Although
Heaven is essence and form,[3] if it does not
follow Tao, it cannot keep its clarity.[4]
Being empty, Tao may be used, and its usefulness cannot be exhausted. Filling it makes
for total capacity, and when that capacity is

reached, there will be overflowing. Truly,
"empty, it may be used," and yet its capacity
is never exhausted. Then its infinity reaches
the highest degree. Although its form is
big, it will not be trouble for the body.
Although there is much to be done, its capacity
cannot be exhausted. When the myriad things
forsake this (Tao) and seek (another) master,
where is another master to be found? Is it
not likewise "bottomless, perhaps the ancestor
of all things"? It blunts the sharpness but
itself is not diminished. The tangles are
untied but it will not tire itself. It softens
the light but does not soil its body. It
becomes one with the dusty world but its true
state will not be changed. Is it not "deep
and still, it appears to exist forever"? If
the Earth keeps its form, then by its virtue
it cannot support more than its capacity. If
Heaven is contented with its forms, then by
its virtue it cannot cover more than its
capacity. If Heaven and Earth cannot be
compared with it (Tao), does it not "seem to
have existed before the Lord"? The Lord (Ti[b])
means the Lord of Heaven.

NOTES

1. Chan's note (p. 106, note 4): The word hsiang[c] here means "seems" and repeats the feeling expressed in the word "appear" two lines before. To interpret it to mean "image" as do Arthur Waley and Duyvendak, or "form"...would be to make the Lao Tzu more metaphysical than it really is.

2. According to Tsukada Taihō and Den Shiryū, erh-i[d] (two molds) here means heaven and earth. However, in Wang Pi, chapter 25, it means having physical form and having no physical form, or original substance and the phenomenal world.

3. Ching-hsiang[e], literally 'psychic phenomenon," means spirit in contrast to hsing-p'o[f] (the physical body).

4. According to Yen Ling-feng, read ching[g] (essence) and ch'ing[h] (clear). In Lao Tzu, chapter 39, it says, "Heaven obtained the One and became clear. Earth obtained the One and became tranquil." Yen also says that the Wang Pi commentary up to this point is originally the commentary on chapter 25. However, Wang Pi often expressed similar ideas in different chapters.

CHAPTER 5

Heaven and Earth are not benevolent.[1]

They regard all things as straw dogs.[2]

Heaven and Earth leave what is natural
(Tzu-jan, Self-so) alone. They do nothing
and create nothing. The myriad things manage
and order themselves. Therefore they are not
benevolent. One who is benevolent will
create things, set things up, bestow benefits
on them and influence them. He gives favors
and does something. When he creates, sets
things up, bestows benefits on things and
influences them, then things will lose their
true being. When he gives favors and does
something, things will no longer exist completely. When things can no longer exist
completely, (heaven and earth) will not be
able to cover[3] and carry everything. Animals
eat straw, though the earth does not produce
it for them. Men eat dogs,[4] though (heaven)
does not produce dogs for them. If nothing
is done to the myriad things, each will accord
with its function, and everything is then
self-sufficient. If one builds up favors,[5]
it will be impossible to leave things alone.

The sage is not benevolent.

He regards all people as straw dogs.

The sage (in his heart) is one with Heaven

and Earth (has character as Heaven and
Earth).[6] For him, people are like straw
and dogs.

How Heaven and Earth are like a bellow!
While vacuous, it is never exhausted.
When active, it produces even more.

T'o[a] is a series of bellows. Yüeh[b] is
comparable to a flute. The inside of the
bellows is empty, without feeling and without
action. Therefore, while vacuous, it can
never be exhausted, and when moved (used),
will never be spent. In the vast and extensive space between heaven and earth they are
left alone. Therefore they, like a bellows,
cannot be exhausted.

Much talk will, of course,[7] come to a dead end.
It is better to keep to the center.

The more one acts, the more one is mistaken.
Things build their evil,[8] and actions bring
about the wrong words. They will not do.[9]
Do not speak.[10] And do not manage.[11]
(Otherwise), one surely comes to a dead end.
If the bellows keeps to the center,[12] there
will be no exhaustion. If one discards oneself
and leaves things alone,[13] then everything will
be in order. If the bellows has an intention
to produce sound, it cannot fulfill[14] the
demand of the blower.

NOTES

1. Chan's translation, "Heaven and Earth are not humane." He noted (p. 108, note 1): Jen[c] (humane) has been variously translated as "love," "benevolence," "human-heartedness," "true manhood," and so on. For a discussion of the translation of this term, see Wing-tsit Chan, A Source Book in Chinese Philosophy, Appendix, "On Translating Certain Chinese Philosophical Terms."

2. Chan's note (p. 108, note 2): Straw dogs were used for sacrifices in ancient China. After they had been used, they were thrown away and there was no more sentimental attachment to them.

3. According to T'ao Hung-ch'ing, pei[d] (to provide, to complete) is to be taken as pei[e] (to cover).

4. Note that Wang Pi differed from Lao Tzu in considering stray dogs as two separate things. It is astonishing how earthly Wang Pi's interpretation is here.

5. Read hui[f] (wisdom) as hui[g] (favor).

6. Book of Changes, commentary on hexagram no. 1, Ch'ien[h] (Heaven).

7. Chan's note (p. 108, note 3): Practically all translators, including Waley and Duyvendak, take shu[i] to mean "quick," "soon," or "much,"....They find little support among Chinese commentators. According to Wang Pi, it means the principle (li[j])

of things, and Ho-shang Kung has followed him. Lu Te-ming quotes Wang Pi and adds the meaning of shih[k] (tendency). In either case it means the course of things, or their history....

8. T'ao Hung-ch'ing suggests to read o[l] (evil) as hui[m] (wisdom) to conform with "wisdom is built up" above.

9. Some words are probably missing in this sentence.

10. Many commentators regard the two words pu-yen[n] (not to speak) as spurious. The passage here is obscure.

11. Li[o] means to manage. Many commentators have tried to make sense out of it.

12. Shu[p] (number, principle) before chung[q] (center) is clearly spurious.

13. A similar statement is found in Wang Pi, chapter 38.

14. Hatano I, p. 70, quoting various Chinese writers, points out that kung[r] (to share) can also be taken as kung[s] (to fulfill, to supply) or as kung[t] (to bow).

CHAPTER 6

The spirit of the valley never dies.

It is called the subtle and profound female.

The gate of the subtle and profound female[1]

Is the root of Heaven and Earth.

It is continuous, and seems to be always existing.

Use it and you will never wear it out.

The spirit of the valley is comparable to the center of the valley which is nothing,[2] without form, without shadow, without opposing it and without going against it. It remains quite low and does not move. It holds on to quietude and does not decline. The valley[3] is formed by it, but we cannot see its form. This is a perfect thing. It remains so low that we cannot name it. Therefore we call it "the root of Heaven and Earth. It is continuous, and seems to be always existing. Use it and you will never wear it out."[4] The gate is whence the subtle and profound (mysterious) female goes through. Following the path which the female takes, it becomes one body with the ultimate.[5] Therefore it is called the root of Heaven and Earth. If we say it exists, we do not see its form. If we say it does not exist, the myriad things come into existence because of it.[6] Therefore "it is continuous and seems to be always existing."

22

It completes all things. Use it, and it is
never burdened. Therefore it is said, "You
will never wear it out."

NOTES

1. Chan's note (p. 111, note 2): The "Hsiang-erh" commentary interprets ku as "passion" and the gate of the female as the female reproductive organ. Significantly, this sexual interpretation has received no support....

2. Yen Ling-feng, citing a Japanese source (see Hatano, I, p. 71), reads ku[a] (valley) as wu[b] (things). It would then read, "There is nothing in it." This whole commentary was quoted by Chang Chan[c] (fl. 320) in his own commentary of the Lieh Tzu[d] (attributed to Lieh Yü-k'ou[e], 450-375 B.C.?), Ssu-pu ts'ung-k'an ed., 1:1b.

3. T'ao Hung-ch'ing substitutes wu for ku, making the sentence to read, "Things are produced by it." In Wang Pi, chapter 41, the sentence is repeated with the word wu.

4. This quotation of the two sentences from the Lao Tzu does not appear in Chang Chan's quotation of the Wang Pi commentary. Both T'ao and Yen therefore think that the quotation should be deleted.

5. Chang Chan has t'ai-chi[f] (great ultimate) instead of simply chi[g] (ultimate). Yen thinks Chang Chan should be followed. However, Chang Chan does not adhere to the Wang Pi commentary strictly.

6. These two sentences, with some variation, also appear in Wang Pi, chapter 14.

CHAPTER 7

Heaven is eternal and Earth everlasting.

They can be eternal and everlasting because they
do not exist for themselves.

If one exists for oneself, one will compete
with others. If one does not exist for oneself,
everything will come to him.

And for this reason can exist forever.

Therefore the sage places himself in the background
but finds himself in the foreground.

He puts himself away, and yet he always remains.

Is it not because he has no personal interests?

This is the reason why his personal interests are
fulfilled.

Having no personal interests means not doing
anything for oneself. One finds himself in
the foreground and always remains. It is
therefore said, "His personal interests can
be fulfilled."

CHAPTER 8

The best (man[1]) is like water.

Water is good; it benefits all things and does not
   compete with them.

It dwells in (lowly) places that all disdain.

   What man hates is lowliness.

This is why it is so near to Tao.

   Tao is nonbeing. Water is being. Therefore
   it is said to be near to (Tao).

(The best man) in his dwelling loves the earth.

In his heart, he loves what is profound.

In his associations, he loves humanity.

In his words, he loves faithfulness.

In government, he loves order.

In handling affairs, he loves competence.

In his activities, he loves timeliness.

It is because he does not compete that he is without
   reproach.

   That means man[2] should always respond to
   this[3] Tao.

NOTES

1. Chan's note (p. 114, note 1): Most commentators and translators have understood the Chinese phrase literally as the highest good, but some commentators and translators have followed Wang Pi and taken the phrase to mean the best man. Both interpretations are possible. The former interpretation has a parallel in chapter 38, which talks about the highest virtue, while the latter has a parallel in chapter 17, where both Wang Pi and Ho-shang Kung interpret "the best" to mean the best ruler. I have followed Wang Pi, not only because his commentary on the text is the oldest and most reliable, but also because the Lao Tzu deals with man's way of life more than abstract ideas.

2. The Tao-te chen-ching chi-chu version has shui[a] (water) instead of jen[b] (man). A number of Chinese and Japanese commentators have followed it. See Hatano, I, p. 77. However, the Lao Tzu also talks about man here.

3. The commentary has chih[c] (order) but some editions, including the Tao-te chen-ching chi-chu, have tz'u[d] (this), which makes better sense. See Hatano, ibid.

CHAPTER 9

To hold and fill a cup to overflowing
Is not as good as to stop in time

> To hold means not to lose the virtue. If
> you (desire) not to lose virtue but wish to
> increase it, it will inevitably collapse.
> Therefore it is not as good as to stop in
> time. That is, it is not so good as to be
> without virtue and to be without accomplishment.

Sharpen a sword-edge to its very sharpest,
And the (edge) will not last long.

> If one sharpens the edge so that it is sharp
> and continues to sharpen it, the edge will
> inevitably be broken. Therefore it will
> not last long.

When gold and jade fill your hall,
You will not be able to keep them.

> It is not as good as to stop in time.

To be proud with honor and wealth
Is to cause one's own downfall.

> That means it will not last long.

Withdraw as soon as your work is done.[1]
Such is Heaven's Way.

> The four seasons rotate. When the work is
> done, they move on.[2]

NOTES

1. Chan's note (p. 115, note 2): The Ho-shang Kung and some fifty other texts, according to Chiang Hsi-ch'ang, have <u>kung-ch'eng ming-sui</u>[a] (work done and fame accomplished). Since this stress on fame does not agree with Taoist philosophy, I have preferred <u>kung-sui</u> (work accomplished) in the Wang Pi text.

2. A paraphrase of a saying by Ts'ai Tse[b] (d. c. 221 B.C.) in <u>Shih-chi</u>[c] (Records of the historian, by Ssu-ma Ch'ien[d], 145-86 B.C.), <u>Ssu-pu ts'ung-k'an</u> edition, 79:17b.

CHAPTER 10

Can you keep[1] the spirit[2] and embrace the One

without departing from them?

To keep[3] is to dwell in it. The spirit is

the eternal abode of man.[4] The One is the true

nature of man. It means that if you can always

dwell in the eternal abode, embrace the One,

keep the spirit clear, and are able never to

depart from them, "all things would submit

spontaneously" (or would be your guests).[5]

Can you concentrate [chuan[a]][6] your vital force and

achieve the highest degree of weakness like

an infant?

To chuan is to employ and to achieve is to

reach the highest degree. It means that if

you employ the vital force of Tzu-jan, achieve

the harmony of the highest degree of weakness,

and are like an infant without desires, things

will be preserved and your nature will be

obtained.

Can you clean and purify your profound insight so

it will be spotless?

What is profound (subtle, mysterious) is the

utmost limit of things. It means that if you

are able to clean and remove evil and falsehood

to arrive at utmost insight[7] and do not let

things restrict your insight or injure your

spirit, you will finally become one with this

profoundness.[8]

Can you love the people and govern the state without knowledge (cunning)?

To use tricks to achieve accomplishment and to manipulate the course of things and thus to seek to escape (from people) is cunning. Profound insight so that it will be spotless means to abandon sageliness. To govern the state without resorting to cunning means to discard wisdom.[9] If you can do it without cunning, people will not avoid you and the government of the state will be in order.

Can you play the role of the female in the opening and closing of the gates of Heaven?[10]

The gates of Heaven is the place through which the world passes. Opening and closing are the juncture of order and disorder. The successive opening and closing prevail over the whole world. Therefore it is said, "The opening and closing of the gates of Heaven." The female responds but does not lead, follows but does not (deliberately) act. It means that if you can play the role of the female in the opening and closing of the gates of Heaven, all things will submit spontaneously[11] and you will live in peace.

Can you understand all and penetrate all without taking any action?

This means that if you understand perfectly
and penetrate all without delusion and are able
not to take any (deliberate) action, then
things will transform (spontaneously). This
is what is meant by saying, "Tao invariably
takes no action. If kings and barons can keep
it, all things will transform spontaneously."[12]

To produce things

That is, not to block their source.

  and to rear them,

That is, not to inhibit their true nature.

To produce, but not to take possession of them,

To act, but not to rely on one's own ability,

To lead them, but not to master them--

This is called profound and secret virtue.

If you do not block the source of things, they
will come into being by themselves. What
achievement is there? If you do not inhibit
the nature of things, things will succeed by
themselves. What action is there to rely on?
Things grow and become proficent by themselves
and I neither master nor complete them. To
have virtue without being a master--is that
not a subtle (profound mystery)? Whenever
one speaks of profound and secret virtue, it
always indicates virtue without our knowing
who the master is. It comes from secret depths.

NOTES

1. Chan's note (p. 117, note 1): Emperor Ming-huang thinks that tsai[b] (to keep) is interchangeable with tsai[c] (a particle for exclamation) and should be the last word of the preceding chapter. [Some] commentators have followed him. Furthermore, they contend, since all lines of this chapter contain four words except this first line, the word tsai must be superfluous to it. However, it is found in both the Wang Pi and Ho-shang Kung texts as well as in their commentaries, and is also found in the passage quoted in the Huai-nan Tzu[d] (by Liu An[e], 179-122 B.C.), Ssu-pu pei-yao[f] (Essentials of the Four Libraries), ed., 12:14a. The phrase tsai ying-p'o[g] appears in a work by Ch'ü Yüan[h] (343-277 B.C.). (See Ch'u tz'u[i] [Elegies of Ch'u], Ssu-pu pei-yao ed., 5:6b.) Furthermore, the two words ying-p'o (the spirit) represent one concept, forming a parallel with the One. Without the word tsai, there would be no verb for "the spirit."

2. Chan's note (p. 117, note 2): Ying-p'o means hun-p'o[j], the heavenly and earthly aspects of the soul. As generally understood, hun is the spirit of man's vital force, expressed in man's intelligence and power of breathing, whereas p'o is the spirit of man's physical nature, expressed

in bodily movement. The "Hsiang-erh" commentary interprets p'o as semen, on the ground that po[k] (white) forms a part of the character p'o and is pronounced like it. Since the "Hsiang-erh" commentary is a Taoist religious text, chiefly concerned with the conservation of human energy in order to prolong life, it has gone so far as to interpret "white" in chapter 28 as semen and "black" as the inside of the female organ, where, it says, it is dark.

3. In the silk manuscript of the Lao Tzu discovered in an ancient tomb at Ma-wang-tui[l], Changsha, in 1974, the word tsai is at the head of the chapter. See Wen-wu[m] (Cultural products) 11 (1974): 12, 18.

4. Chu Hsi[n] (1130-1200) severely criticized this interpretation as "nonesense." To him, the sentence merely means what it says. (Chu Tzu yü-lei[o] (Classified conversations of Master Chu), 1880 ed., 137:5a, but Wang Pi was expounding his own philosophy.

5. Literally, "All will naturally be your guests." Compare Lao Tzu, chapter 32: "Tao is eternal and has no name. Though its simplicity seems insignificant, none in the world can master it. If kings and barons would hold on to it, all things would submit to them spontaneously."

6. Chan's note (p. 117, note 3): Chuan means neither ["to follow"] as Wang Pi thinks, nor "to

employ," as Ho-shang Kung thinks, but "to concentrate," according to Chu Hsi. See Chu Tzu yü-lei,
125:10a.

7. In version B of the silk manuscript of the
Lao Tzu, the word is chien[p], meaning a mirror (to
look at a pool of water to see one's own reflection),
and in version A it is lan[q] (blue), a corruption
of chien. See Wen-wu, 11, 18 and 12, respectively.

8. Compare Lao Tzu, chapter 56: "He who knows
does not speak. He who speaks does not know. Close
the mouth. Shut the doors. Blunt the sharpness.
Untie the tangles. Soften the light. Become one
with the dusty world. This is called profound
identification."

9. Compare Lao Tzu, chapter 19: "Abandon
sageliness and discard wisdom; then the people will
benefit a hundredfold."

10. Chan's note (p. 118, note 8): Ho-shang
Kung says the heavenly gates refer to the place in
the Polar Star where the Lord of Heaven is. He
is definitely confusing Taoist philosophy with later
Taoist religion. Modern writers have explained it
in terms of the senses, or specifically the ears,
mouth, and nose, or the alternation of activity and
tranquility in the operation of Nature, or the
spiritual and mental activities of man. Most writers,
however, are satisfied with Wang Pi's explanation
that which means the way of Nature. In the Chuang Tzu
chapter 23 (8:13b), it means "non-being," In his

commentary on the passage in the Chuang Tzu.

Kuo Hsiang[r] (d. 312) says that the gate of Heaven is a general name for all things and that it is the same as "the door of all subtleties" in chapter 1 of the Lao Tzu....Waley thinks p'o is literally "semen" and that "opening and closing" alludes to a sexual technique.

11. Compare Lao Tzu, chapter 32.

12. This sentence appears in Lao Tzu, chapter 37.

CHAPTER 11

Thirty spokes are united around the hub to make a
wheel,

But it is on its nonbeing that the utility of the
carriage depends.

The reason why the hub unites and controls or
leads thirty spokes is due to its nonbeing.
Because of its nonbeing, it can accept all.
It really[1] guides all.

Clay is molded to form a utensil,

But it is on its nonbeing that the utility of the
utensil depends.

Doors and windows are cut out to make a room,

But it is on its nonbeing that the utility of the
room depends.

Therefore turn being into advantage, and turn
nonbeing into utility.

The reason why wood, clay, and wall can make
these three things is because all function
through their nonbeing. Nonbeing means to
turn being into advantage. They all rely on
nonbeing to be useful (to function).[2]

NOTES

1. Here commentators are unclear. Various suggestions have been made to read shih[a] (really) as shih[b] (is), kua[c] (few), and chih[d] (perfect). See Hatano, I, p. 92.

2. A similar sentence appears in Wang Pi, chapter 1, translated there as: To be useful, it has to function through nonbeing. It also appears in Wang Pi, chapter 40.

CHAPTER 12

The five colors[1] cause one's eyes to be blind.

The five tones cause one's ears to be deaf.

The five flavors cause one's palate to be spoiled.

Racing and hunting cause one's mind to be mad.

> To be spoiled means something has gone wrong.
> It is said to be spoiled because the function
> of the mouth has been lost. Ears, eyes,
> mouth (palate), and heart should all follow
> their own nature. If one does not use them
> to accord with his nature and destiny but
> instead to injure his just-so-ness (Tzu-jan),
> then one is said to be deaf, blind, spoiled,
> and mad.

Goods that are hard to get injure one's activities.

> Goods that are hard to get obstruct one's
> direct road (and) therefore injure one's
> activities.

For this reason the sage is concerned with the belly
and not the eyes.

Therefore he rejects the one but accepts the other.

> Being concerned with the belly means to nourish
> oneself with things. Being concerned with the
> eyes means to enslave oneself by things. For
> this reason the sage is not concerned with
> the eyes.

NOTES

1. Chan's note (p. 121, note 1): The five colors are blue, yellow, red, white, and black; the five sounds, the five full tones in the Chinese musical scale; the five tastes, salty, bitter, sour, acrid, and sweet. These fivefold classifications have resulted from the theory of Five Agents or Elements, which conceives things to be results of the interactions of the Five Agents, namely, Water, Fire, Wood, Metal, and Earth. Many things have been formed in sets of five to correspond to them.

CHAPTER 13

Be apprehensive when receiving favor or disgrace.

Regard great trouble as seriously as you regard
your body.

What is meant by being apprehensive when receiving
favor or disgrace?

Favor is considered inferior.

Be apprehensive when you receive them and also be
apprehensive when you lose them.

This is what is meant by being apprehensive when
receiving favor or disgrace.

Favor is certainly followed by disgrace and
honor is certainly followed by trouble.
Favor[1] and disgrace are equal, and honor and
trouble are the same. If a subject is
apprehensive when receiving favor,[2] disgrace,
honor, or trouble, he cannot be trusted with
the empire.

What does it mean to regard great trouble as
seriously as you regard the body?
Great trouble belongs to the same category as
honor and favor. "The fulness of life leads
surely to death."[3] Therefore it is called
"great trouble." When one is deluded by honor
and favor, (the effect) will fall back on the
person. Therefore it is said that the great
trouble is (to be regarded) as one's body
(person).

The reason why I have great trouble is that I have
a body.

(Trouble) arises because I have a body.

If I have no body,

(because of) the return to Tzu-jan.

What trouble could I have?

Therefore he who values the world as his body may
be entrusted with the empire.

Nothing can change the body. Therefore it is
said to regard it seriously. Only when one
does so can he be entrusted with the empire.

He who loves the world as his body may be entrusted
with the empire.

Nothing can hurt the body. Therefore it is
said to love it. Only when one does so can
he be entrusted with the empire. Only when one
neither hurts nor changes his body with favor,
disgrace, honor, or trouble can one be entrusted
with the empire.

NOTES

1. The <u>Lao Tzu</u> text has <u>ching</u>[a] (apprehensive),
but as many writers have pointed out, judged by the
preceding sentences, <u>ching</u> is obviously a misprint
for <u>ch'ung</u>[b] (favor).

2. Chan's note (p. 123, note 3): Wang Pi's
text has: "favor is inferior" and the expression
can be understood as favor received by those in
inferior positions. Wang Pi has commented on it in
this sense. Ho-shang Kung, on the other hand, has
"disgrace is inferior." According to Chiang Hsi-
ch'ang, nine other texts agree with Ho-shang Kung.
Thirty-two have "favor is inferior" and six have
"favor is superior and disgrace inferior."

3. Compare <u>Lao Tzu</u>, chapter 50.

CHAPTER 14

We look at it and do not see it;

Its name is The Invisible.

We listen to it and do not hear it;

Its name is The Inaudible.

We touch it and do not find it;

Its name is The Subtle (formless).[1]

These three cannot be further inquired into,

And hence merge into one.

Because it has no shape, no form, no sound,
and no echo, there is nothing it cannot
penetrate and nowhere it cannot go. It cannot
be known. Furthermore, I do not know its
name[2] by my ears, eyes, or body. Therefore
they cannot further be inquired into, and
hence merge into one.

Going up high, it is not bright, and coming down

low, it is not dark.

Infinite and boundless, it cannot be given any name;

It reverts to nothingness.

This is called shape without shape,

Form without objects.

If we say it does not exist, the myriad things
come to completion because of it. If we say
it exists, we do not see its form.[3] Therefore
it is said, "Shape without shape. Form without
objects."

It is The Vague and Elusive.

It is indefinable.

Meet it and you will not see its head.

Follow it and you will not see its back.

Hold on to the Tao of old in order to master the
things of the present.

Things (affairs) means events that take place.

From this one may know the primeval beginning (of
the universe).

This is called the bond^4 of Tao.

The formless and nameless is the ancestor of
the myriad things. Although present and past
are not the same, time changes, and customs
alter, yet through it all things fully obtain
their order.^{5} Therefore it is possible to "hold
on to the Tao of old in order to master the
things of the present." Although antiquity
is far away, its Tao still exists. Therefore,
though we are in the present, we can know the
primeval beginning.

NOTES

1. Chan's note (p. 125, note 7): The Doctrine of the Mean, chapters 1, 33.

2. Yen Ling-feng suggests that ming[a] (name) should read ho[b] (what?), that is, what it is.

3. The two sentences also appear in Wang Pi, chapter 6.

4. Chan's note (p. 125, note 8): Ch'eng I[c] (1033-1107), Preface to the I chuan[d] (Commentary on the Book of Changes).

5. Yen argues that chih[e] (order) should be read shih[f] (beginning) to conform with "beginning" at the end of the commentary.

CHAPTER 15

Of old those who were the best rulers were subtly

mysterious and profoundly penetrating;

Too deep to comprehend.

And because they cannot be comprehended,

I can only describe them arbitrarily:

Cautious like crossing a frozen stream in the winter,

Cautious like crossing a frozen stream in the

winter, as though they wished and yet did not

wish to go over. Their feeling is impossible

to perceive.

Being at a loss, like one fearing danger on all sides,

When the four neighbors (all sides) attack,

the master of the center is at a loss and does

not know in what direction to go. The clues

of people of high virtue cannot be seen, and

their intentions[1] cannot be known. They also

are like these (two examples).

Reserved, like one visiting,[2]

Supple and pliant, like ice about to melt,

Genuine, like a piece of uncarved wood,

Open and broad, like a valley,

Merged and indifferentiated, like muddy water.[3]

The word "like" in these sentences mean that

appearances and forms in these cases are not

describable.

Who can make muddy water gradually clear through

tranquility?

Who can make the still gradually come to life through

   activity?

   Through principle (li^a), obscure things become

   brilliant. Through tranquility, muddy things

   become clear. Through activity, still things

   will come to life. This is the Tao of Tzu-jan.

   "He who makes...?" describes the difficulty of

   the task. "Gradually" means thoroughness and

   caution.

He who embraces this Tao does not want to fill

   himself to overflowing.

   "Fill to overflowing" means that it will

   certainly go over the brim.

It is precisely because there is no overflowing

   that he is beyond wearing out and renewal.

   Pi means to cover.[4]

48

NOTES

1. This sentence also appears in Wang Pi, chapter 17. There te-ch'ü[b] (virtue-interest) reads i-ch'ü[c] (intention). According to T'ao Hung-ch'ing, te-ch'ü here should read i-ch'ü also.

2. Chan's note (p. 127, note 3): Jung[d] (appearance, attitude) in the Wang Pi text but k'o[e] (guest) in the Ho-shang Kung, Fu I, and fifty-one other texts mentioned by Chiang Hsi-ch'ang. K'o rhymes with the four following lines; jung does not. It is interesting that Waley has written a long commentary on jung (for this chapter), but chooses k'o here instead of jung.

3. Chan's note (p. 127, note 4): The sevenfold description may suggest a progression, or seven categories of moral cultivation, but there is no need to treat the Lao Tzu so systematically.

4. Most commentators feel that Wang Pi's interpretation of pi[f] as "to cover" does not make sense and that pi here is the same as pi[g] (worn out) in Lao Tzu, chapter 22.

CHAPTER 16

Attain complete vacuity.

Maintain steadfast quietude.

>This is to say that attaining vacuity is the utmost steadfastness (seriousness) of things, and maintaining quietude is the true correctness of things.

All things come into being,

>That is, to be active and to grow.

And I see thereby their return.

>The return is to be seen in vacuity and quietude. Being arises out of vacuity and movement arises out of quietude. Therefore although the myriad things act together, finally they will return to vacuity and quietude. That is the ultimate steadfastness of things.

All things flourish,

But each one returns to its root.

>Each thing returns to its origin.

This return to its root means tranquility.

It is called returning to its destiny.

To return to destiny is called the eternal (Tao).

>If one returns to one's root, one will be tranquil. Therefore it is called tranquility. When one is tranquil, one returns to one's destiny. Therefore it is called returning to one's destiny. When one returns to one's destiny, one attains the eternity of nature

and destiny. Therefore it is called the
eternal.

To know the eternal is called enlightenment.

Not to know the eternal is to act blindly to
result in disaster. This thing called eternal
is neither partial nor prominent.[1] There is
no appearance of light or darkness and no
manifestation of heat or cold. Therefore it
is said, "To know the eternal is called enlightenment." Only by this return can one
embrace and penetrate all things so that nothing
is not contained. If one is mistaken from this
point on, evil enters into one's lot and things
will be separated from their lot[2] (nature).
Therefore it is said, "Not to know the eternal
is to act blindly to result in disaster."

He who knows the eternal is all-embracing.

There is nothing that is not embraced or
penetrated.

Being all-embracing, he is impartial.

When he embraces and penetrates everything, he
reaches the point of complete impartiality.

Being impartial, he is kingly (universal).[3]

When he is completely impartial, he reaches
the point of universality.

Being kingly, he is one with Nature.

When he is universal, he will reach the point
of forming a unity with Heaven (Nature).

Being one with Nature, he is in accord with Tao.

When he becomes one with Heaven in virtue,[4]

embracing Tao and becoming pervasive, he will

reach the point of achieving extreme[5] vacuity

and nothingness.

Being in accord with Tao, he is everlasting.

When he achieves vacuity and nothingness to

the infinite and extreme degree and attains the

eternal of Tao, he will reach the point of

having no limit.

And is free from danger throughout his lifetime.

This thing called nonbeing cannot be hurt by

water or fire, or destroyed by metal or stone.

If one exercises it in the mind, the tiger

cannot bite its teeth, and the wild buffalo

cannot butt its horns, and weapons of war

cannot thrust their blades into him.[6] Where

would there be any danger?

52

NOTES

1. The same phrase appears in Wang Pi, chapter 35.

2. $\underline{Fen}^a$ (lot, part, or to divide) hardly makes sense here. T'ao Hung-ch'ing suggests that $\underline{fen}$ in the first instance should read $\underline{chih}^b$ (knowledge) and Yen Ling-feng suggests that $\underline{fen}$ in the second instance should read $\underline{chen}^c$ (true). The idea of $\underline{fen}$ (part or lot) appears in Wang Pi, chapters 25 and 41.

3. Chan's note (p. 129, note 2): "[Some texts] have $\underline{sheng}^d$ (to produce) instead of $\underline{wang}$ (kingly) . . . . Ma Hsü-lun thinks that $\underline{sheng}$ is a corruption of $\underline{wang}^e$, which in turn is a corruption of $\underline{chou}^f$ (universal...."

4. Book of Changes, commentary on hexagram number 1, $\underline{Ch'ien}^g$: "The great man accords in his character with Heaven and Earth." Compare Wang Pi, chapter 5.

5. According to T'ao, $\underline{chi}^h$ (extreme) should read $\underline{ch'iung-chi}^i$ (infinite and extreme) as in the following sentence.

6. Paraphrasing Lao Tzu, chapter 50.

CHAPTER 17

The best[1] (rulers) are those whose existence is
(merely) known by the people.[2]

The best rulers are great men.[3] The great men
are above, Therefore it is said that (they are)
the best rulers. The rulers are really above.
They dwell in "managing affairs without action
and spread doctrines without words.[4] All
things arise, and they do not claim to be their
source." Therefore people merely know that
they exist. That means they follow the rulers
above.

The next best are those who are loved and praised.

(Although the rulers above) cannot manage
affairs without taking action or spread doctrines
without words, they establish the good things
and spread them among the people so that people
below love and praise them.

The next are those who are feared.

They can no longer command things by grace and
benevolence but rely on force and power.

And the next are those who are despised.

They cannot regulate[5] people in the correct
way but govern the empire by strategy (cunning).
The people know how to avoid them, and their
orders are not followed. Therefore it is said
that they are despised.

It is only when one does not have enough faith in

others that others will have no faith in him.
If one does not control one's body in accordance
with nature, then one becomes ill. If one does
not help a thing according to its true being,
then evil flaws and quarrels arise. "It is
only when one does not have enough faith in
others that others will have no faith in him."
This is the Tao of Tzu-jan. When this insufficiency is already felt, there is nothing
which could be accomplished by strategy
(completely).

(The great rulers) value their words highly.
They accomplish their task; they complete their work.
Nevertheless their people say that they simply
follow Nature.

The beginning of Tzu-jan and the omens are not
visible. The intentions (of the great rulers)
cannot be seen.[6] There is nothing which could
change their words, for if they speak, there
will certainly be response. Therefore it is
said, "They value their words highly." They
"manage affairs without action and spread
doctrines without words." They establish things
without forms. Therefore "they accomplish
their task; they complete their work" and people
do not know why this is so.

NOTES

1. Chan's note (p. 130, note 1): T'ai-shang[a] [the highest] is understood by Ho-shang Kung as the highest in time, that is, antiquity, but by most others as the highest in virtue.

2. Chan's note (p. 130, note 2): [Some texts] have pu[b] (not) instead of hsia[c] (people). [Another text] has hsia-pu. In these cases the meaning is that the people did not know of the existence of their government. This version has been accepted by some modern scholars and translators.

3. T'ai-shang can mean either "great antiquity" or "great men on high". In view of what follows in Lao Tzu, Wang Pi's interpretation is correct.

4. Compare Lao Tzu, chapters 2 and 43. A similar statement is found in Wang Pi, chapters 23 and 63.

5. The word fa[d] (law) is superfluous, most scholars agree.

6. Similar ideas are expressed in Wang Pi, chapter 15.

CHAPTER 18

When the great Tao declined,

The doctrine of humanity and righteousness arose.

If one has lost the state of taking no action

and, furthermore, establishes the good[1] by

using strategy, that means[2] pushing things.

When knowledge and wisdom appeared,

There emerged great hypocrisy.

If one applies methods and uses intelligence

to identify the treacherous, his intentions

can be observed and his form (appearance)

can be seen. People will know and avoid him.

Therefore when knowledge and wisdom appear, the

great hypocrisy emerges.

When the six family relationships are not in harmony,

There will be the advocacy of filial piety and deep

love to children.

When a country is in disorder,

There will be the praise of loyal ministers.

Out of great evil arises the name of the

highest good, as it is said that good and evil

belong in the same family.[3] The six family

relationships are: father and son,[4] elder

and younger brothers, and husband and wife.

If these six relationships are naturally in

harmony, and if the empire is naturally in

complete order, then one does not know where

filial piety, deep love for children, and loyal

ministers are to be found. If the fishes
forget the Tao of rivers and lakes,[5] then
the need (virtue) to help each other arises.

NOTES

1. Compare Wang Pi, chapter 5, commentary on
the first two lines of Lao Tzu, chapter 5.

2. Hatano, I, p. 127, says that the character
tao[a] got into the text by mistake because it
resembles the character chin[b] (to advance, to
push), but it can mean "it means" here.

3. Compare Wang Pi, chapter 2.

4. Certain editions have "mother" but that
would duplicate the relationship of husband and
wife and omit the relationship of parents and
children.

5. Quoting Chuang Tzu, chapter 6 (3:8b).

CHAPTER 19

Abandon sageliness and discard wisdom;

Then the people will benefit a hundredfold.

Abandon humanity and discard righteousness;

Then the people will return to filial piety and

deep love.

Abandon skill and discard profit;

Then there will be no thieves or robbers.

However, these three things are ornaments $(\underline{wen}^a)$ [1]

and are not adequate.

Therefore let people hold on to these:

Manifest plainness,

Embrace simplicity,

Reduce selfishness,

Have few desires.

Sageliness and wisdom are the benison[2] in a

talent. Humanity and righteousness are the

benison in a human being. Skill and benefit

are the benison in a function. And yet the

text just says to abandon them. Ornaments

are greatly inadequate. If people are not

enabled to hold on to something, there is

nothing by which they will perceive the

fundamentals. Therefore it is said, "These

three things are ornaments and are not adequate."

Hence let people hold on to something: hold on

to plainness, simplicity, and having few desires.

NOTES

1. Chan's note (p. 132, note 2): The word _wen_ has many meanings--adornment, culture, literature, social systems, education, words, argument, superficiality, artificiality, grain, pattern, and so on--and has led to various translations, perhaps more diverse than any other word.

2. One edition has _chieh_[b] (outstanding) instead of _shan_[c] (good, praiseworthy, benison).

CHAPTER 20

Abandon learning and there will be no sorrow.[1]

How much difference is there between "Yes, sir," and
"Of course not"?

How much difference is there between "good" and
"evil"?

What people dread, do not fail to dread.

In Part II (it is said), "The pursuit of learning
is to increase day after day. The pursuit of
Tao is to decrease day after day."[2] This
being the case, learning is to increase one's
ability and to improve one's knowledge. If
we are without desires and are content, why
should we seek to increase our knowledge? If
we reach (hit) the target without knowledge,
why then pursue progress? Swallows have mates
and doves have companions.[3] People who live
in cold places naturally know the particular
furs. Thus that which is natural suffices,
and to exceed it will cause trouble. Thus to
lengthen the feet of the duck is not different
from cutting the skin bone of the crane.[4] If
one wishes to advance out of fear[5] for one's
reputation, how does that differ from fearing
punishment? "Yes, sir," and "Of course not,"
"good" and "evil"--how far do they differ?
Therefore what people dread, I dread also. I
dare not depend on that in order to become

useful.

But, alas, how confused, and the end is not yet.[6]

I sigh that I differ so much from the vulgar
or ordinary person.

The multitude are merry, as though feasting on a
day of sacrifice.

Or like ascending a tower in the springtime.

The multitude are deluded by beauty and progress
and become influenced (confused) by glory and
profit. They want to advance and rival in
their hearts. Therefore "the multitude are
merry, as though feasting on a day of sacrifice. Or like ascending a tower in the
springtime."

I alone am inert, showing no sign (of desires),

Like an infant that has not yet smiled.

That is, I am empty; I have no form one can
put a name to and no noticeable signs that can
be indicated, "like an infant that has not yet
smiled."

Wearied, indeed, I seem to be without a home.

As though I were homeless.

The multitude all possess more than enough.

I alone seem to have lost all.

The multitude have things they cherish. They
have designs (thoughts, ambitions), and thus
the whole heart is filled to overflowing.
Therefore it is said, "The multitude all
possess more than enough." I alone am empty,

without action, without desires, as though I
would lose (everything).

Mine is indeed the mind of an ignorant man,

> In the heart of absolutely ignorant people,
> there is no place in which to make any dis-
> tinction. In their reflections (thoughts),
> there is neither wish nor desire. Since that
> is so, these feelings cannot be discerned.
> I am like this, as though falling in completely.

Indiscriminate and dull!

> As there is nothing that I would discriminate,
> there is nothing to be named.[7]

Common folk are indeed brilliant;

> That is, they let their brightness dazzle.

I alone seem to be in the dark.

Common folk see differences and are clear-cut;

> That means to differentiate and analyze (to
> make distinctions).

I alone make no distinctions.

I seem drifting as the sea;

> The feelings are invisible.

Like the wind blowing about, seemingly without

> destination.
> There is nothing that can be caught hold of
> and held on to.

The multitude all have a purpose;

> That means (all) have a function; all long for
> application and function.

I alone seem to be stubborn and rustic.

If there is nothing I would like to do, I am

closed (making no distinctions) and dark as

though I knew nothing. Therefore one speaks

of being stubborn and, moreover, rustic.

I alone differ from others.

And value drawing sustenance from Mother (Tao)

Drawing sustenance from Mother is the root of

life. All others reject the root which gives

life to people, but honor the flower or

unimportant ornaments. Therefore it is said,

"I alone differ from others."

NOTES

1. Chan's note (p. 135, note 1): This line is definitely out of place here. Because it rhymed in ancient times with the last two lines of the preceding chapter, because like them it contains four words, and because it expresses a similar idea, many scholars...have shifted it to the end of the last chapter.....[Others]...have transferred it to the beginning of the preceding chapter, for the reason that like the first three sentences it begins with "abandon."...

2. Quoting Lao Tzu, chapter 48.

3. This may be a quotation, but it is not found in the Thirteen Confucian Classics or the Chuang Tzu.

4. Quoting Chuang Tzu, chapter 8 (4:4a).

5. To stand in awe of fame.

6. Chan's note (p. 135, note 2): Yang[a] literally means "dawn," but it also means "the end," "limit," "to stop," and so on.

7. Read ming[b] (bright) as ming[c] (name), according to several old editions. See Hatano, I, p. 143.

CHAPTER 21

The all-embracing quality of the great[1] virtue
follows alone from the Tao.

K'ung[a] (great) means empty. Only if one
considers emptiness as a virtue can one in one's
activities follow Tao.

The thing that is called Tao is eluding and vague.

Eluding and vague is the description[2] of that
being which is without form and without
attachment.

Vague and eluding, there is in it the form.

Eluding and vague, in it are things.

In formlessness, things begin; by being
unattached, things are accomplished. The myriad
things begin and are accomplished in this way
and we do not know why this is so. Therefore
it is said, "Vague and eluding, eluding and
vague, there is in it the form."

Deep and obscure, in it is the essence.

"Deep and obscure" is the description[3] of depth
and distance. As it is deep and distant, we
cannot see it. But the myriad things follow
it, and thus it can be seen, and its truth
(reality) can be determined. Therefore it is
said, "Deep and obscure, in it is the essence."

The essence is very real; in it are evidences.

Evidences mean proof. If things return to depth
and to obscurity, then the ultimate of true

essence can be obtained and the nature (reality) of the myriad things can be determined. Therefore it is said, "The essence is very real, in it are evidences."

From the time of old until now, its name (manifestations) ever remains.

The ultimate of perfect truth is unnameable. "Nameless" is its name. From the time of old until now, there is nothing which does not reach completion in this way. Therefore it is said, "From the time of old until now, its name ever remains."

By which we may see the beginning of all things.

The beginning of all things means the onset of (all) things. Here the nameless is used to explain[4] the beginning of all things.

How do I know that the beginnings of all things are so?

Through this (Tao).

This is what is said above. It means: How do I know that the beginning of all things arises out of nonbeing? Through this (Tao) I know.

NOTES

1. Wang Pi speaks here of empty virtue.

2. The Wang Pi text has t'an^b (to sigh), a misprint, according to some scholars, for mao^c (appearance). See Hatano, II, p. 2.

3. See note 2.

4. According to Chang Hsi-ch'ang, shuo^d (to explain) here was originally yüeh^e (to see) used in the Lao Tzu text but the meaning of both words is the same. Yen Ling-feng has followed him.

CHAPTER 22

To yield is to be preserved whole.

    If one does not show oneself, his brilliance
will be preserved.

To be bent is to become straight.

    If one does not justify oneself, one's
justification will be prominent.

To be empty is to be full.

    If one does not boast, credit will be given him.

To be worn out is to be renewed.

    If one does not brag, one's virtue will endure
for long.[1]

To have little is to possess.

To have plenty is to be perplexed.

    The Tao of Tzu-jan is like a tree. The more
it grows (to have plenty), the more distant
it is from the roots; the less it grows (to
have little), the less distant it is from the
roots. If one always increases, then one
becomes removed from the true essence. Therefore it is said to be perplexed. If there is
little, one reaches one's roots. Therefore
it is said to possess.

Therefore the sage embraces the One

And becomes the model of the world.

    The One means the ultimate of the little. A
model implies something to follow.

He does not show himself; therefore he is luminous.

He does not justify himself; therefore he becomes
    prominent.

He does not boast of himself; therefore he is
    given credit.

He does not brag; therefore he can endure for long.

It is precisely because he does not compete that
    the world cannot compete with him.

Is the ancient saying, "To yield is to be preserved
    whole," empty words?

Truly he will be preserved and (prominence and
    credit) will come to him.

NOTES

1. Compare this and the three preceding
comments with similar statements in Lao Tzu,
chapter 24.

CHAPTER 23

Nature says few words.

> "We listen to it and do not hear it; its name
> is The Inaudible."[1] In a later chapter it is
> said, "But the words uttered by Tao, how
> insipid and tasteless! We look at it; it is
> inperceptible. We listen to it; it is inau-
> dible."[2] If that is so, then there are (words)
> without taste and one cannot actually hear them.
> These are then perfect words of Tzu-jan.

For the same reason a whirlwind does not last a whole
> morning.

Nor does a rainstorm last a whole day.

What causes them?

It is Heaven and Earth (Nature).

If even Heaven and Earth cannot make them last long,

How much less can man?

> It means that whatever rises violently and
> suddenly[3] will not last long.

Therefore he who follows Tao is identified with Tao.

> To follow means to do, which means that all
> activities follow Tao; Tao accomplishes and
> orders the myriad things by the formless and
> by taking no action. Therefore those who follow
> Tao consider taking no action as the master[4]
> and they teach without words.[5] "It is contin-
> uous, and seems to be always existing."[6] and
> things obtain their true (essence) and will

have the same substance[7] with Tao. Therefore
it is said to be identified with Tao.

He who follows virtue is identified with virtue.
Virtue[8] means little.[9] "To have little is to
possess (have virtue)."˙ Therefore it is said
to have virtue. If one acts virtuously, then
one will have the same substance with virtue.
Therefore it is said to be identified with
virtue.

He who abandons (Tao) is identified with the
abandonment (of Tao).
To abandon (to lose) means to have much trouble.
If you have too much trouble, you will lose.
Therefore it is said to lose. If one acts with
abandonment, then one will have the same
substance with abandonment. Therefore it is
said to be identified with abandonment.

He who is identified with Tao--Tao is also happy to
have him.

He who is identified with virtue--virtue is also
happy to have him.

And he who is identified with the abandonment (of
Tao)--the abandonment (of Tao) is also happy
to abandon him.
This means that whatever you follow in your
acts will respond to and be identified with
you.

72

It is only when one does not have enough faith in
others that others will have no faith in him.
"If you are not loyal and faithful enough to
people below you, they will not trust you."[10]

NOTES

1. Quoting Lao Tzu, chapter 14.

2. Quoting Lao Tzu, chapter 35.

3. Following this, there is the word mei[a]
which in its ordinary meaning of "beautiful" or
"to praise" does not make sense here. Commentators
have substituted for it with various words without
any real improvement. Others say the word is
spurious. See Hatano, II, p. 13.

4. Here we have i wu-wei wei chün[b] (considering
taking no action as the master). In Wang Pi, chapter 63, we have i wu-wei wei chü[c] (dwelling in taking
no action). Pointing this out, Chiang Hsi-ch'ang
says chün should be read chü. See similar statements
in Wang Pi, chapter 17 and compare Lao Tzu,
chapters 2 and 43.

5. Quoting Lao Tzu, chapter 43.

6. Quoting Lao Tzu, chapter 6.

7. The word here is t'i[d] (substance or having
the same substance), a very important concept
in Wang Pi.

8. $\underline{Te}^e$ (to obtain) and $\underline{te}^f$ (virtue) are interchangeable.

9. This sentence makes no sense, but the following sentence in quotation marks appears in Lao Tzu, chapter 22. There Wang Pi's comment says literally, "The less it has, the more it obtains (gets to) the root," meaning that the less it grows, the less distant it is from the root.

10. Paraphrasing Lao Tzu, chapter 17.

CHAPTER 24

He who stands on tiptoe is not steady.

If one esteems advancement, then one loses
serenity. Therefore it is said, "He who stands
on tiptoe is not steady."

He who strides forward does not go.

He who shows himself is not luminous.

He who justifies himself is not prominent.

He who boasts of himself is not given credit.

He who brags does not endure for long.

From the point of view of Tao, these are like
remnants of food and tumors of action.

Looked at as if by Tao, the conduct of Chüeh
Chih[al] was like what is left over after a
big meal. Although in itself beautiful,
it is nevertheless rotten. Although originally
successful, if one boasts, then it is as though
one had a tumor.

Which all creatures detest.

Therefore those who possess Tao turn away from them.

NOTE

1. Chüeh Chih, chief officer of the feudal
state of Chin[b], boasted that none equaled him in
faithfulness, wisdom, and courage. See Tso-chuan[c]
(Tso's commentary, by Tso Ch'iu-ming[d], 6th century
B.C.), Duke Ch'eng[e], 16th year, (603 B.C.), sec.
11, and Shih-chi, 39:35b-36a.

CHAPTER 25

There was something undifferentiated and yet

　complete,

Which existed before heaven and earth.

　Undifferentiated, it is not knowable, but the

　myriad things become complete because of it.

　Therefore it is said, "Undifferentiated and

　yet complete," "I do not know whose son it

　is,"[1] and therefore (it seems) to have existed

　before heaven and earth.

Soundless and formless, it depends on nothing and

　does not change.

　Soundless and formless means being without form

　or body, and nothing can be compared to it.

　Therefore it is said, "It depends on nothing."

　Returning and changing, beginning and ending,

　it does not lose its constancy. Therefore it

　is said, "It does not change."

It operates everywhere and is free from danger.

It may be considered the mother of the universe.

　It operates everywhere and reaches everywhere

　but avoids the danger.[2] That means it can live

　and preserve its great form. Therefore it may

　be considered the mother of the universe.

I do not know its name;

　A name determines a form. What is undifferen-

　tiated, complete, and formless cannot be

　determined. Therefore it is said, "I do not

know its name."

I call it Tao.

> A name is to determine a form, and to call it
> so is to give a name to that which can be named.
> The name Tao is chosen because nothing does not
> go through it.[3] This (Tao) is the greatest of
> the nameable (apparition) among the undifferen-
> tiated and yet complete.

If forced to give it a name, I shall call it Great.

> The reason I call it Tao is because I chose the
> greatest from all that can be used as a name.
> If you inquire into the reason of how the term
> is determined, the answer is that it is attached
> to the great. Whatever is attached to the
> great necessarily has its limited part or lot.
> Having its limited part or lot, it loses its
> ultimate. Therefore, it is said, "If forced
> to give it a name, I shall call it Great."

Now being great means functioning everywhere.

> Functioning everywhere means to go on and not
> to hold on to any great substance. Yet it has
> already operated everywhere and reached every-
> thing. Therefore it is said to be functioning
> everywhere.

Functioning everywhere means far-reaching.

Being far-reaching means returning to the original
point.

> Being far-reaching means the ultimate. It
> reaches everywhere and reaches every limit, and

is not confined to one function. Therefore
it is said to be far-reaching. It does not
follow wherever it goes, because its substance
is independent. Therefore it is said to
return to the original point.
Therefore Tao is great.
Heaven is great.
Earth is great.
And the king[4] is also great.

In the nature of Heaven and Earth, the human
being is the most valuable,[5] and the king is
the master of men. Although his position is
not great, he is still great. He is the match
of the three. Therefore it is said, "The
king is also great."
There are four great things in the universe,
The four great things are Tao, Heaven, Earth,
and the king. Whenever a thing is callable or
nameable, then (what is named) is not its
ultimate. If one calls it Tao, it is because
things come from it.[6] Because things come
from it, we call it Tao. This is what is great
in the nameable, but it is not as good as what
is great in the unnameable. What is uncallable
cannot be named. [We reluctantly] call it
universe. Tao, Heaven, Earth, and the king are
all within the unnameable. Therefore it is
said, "There are four great things in the
universe."

And the king is one of them.

He is great as the master of men.

Man models himself after Earth.

Earth models itself after Heaven.

Heaven models itself after Tao.

And Tao models itself after Nature [Tzu-jan].

To model means to follow. Man does not oppose
Earth and therefore can comfort all things,
for his standard is the Earth. Earth does not
oppose Heaven and therefore can sustain all
things, for its standard is Heaven. Heaven
does not oppose Tao and therefore can cover
all things, for its standard is Tao.[7] Tao does
not oppose Tzu-jan and therefore it attains
its nature. To follow Nature as its standard
is to model after the square while within the
square and the circle while within the circle,
and not to oppose Nature in any way. By Nature
is meant something that cannot be labeled and
something ultimate. To use knowledge is not
as good as to have no knowledge. Body and soul
are not as good as essence and form. Essence
and form are not as good as the formless. That
with modes is not as good as that without modes.[8]
Hence these model after one another. Because
Tao obeys Nature, Heaven relies on it. Because
Heaven models after Tao, Earth follows Heaven
as its principle. Because Earth models after

Heaven, man uses Earth as his form,[9]

and thus becomes the master. The master

is the one who combines things as One.

NOTES

1. Quoting Lao Tzu, chapter 4.

2. Read shih[a] (beginning) as tai[b] (danger).
Shih is clearly a misprint.

3. Compare Wang Pi, chapter 51.

4. Chan's note (p. 145, note 1): [some texts]
have "man" in place of "king." This substitution
has been accepted by Ma Hsü-lun [and others]. They
have been influenced, undoubtedly, by the concept
of the trinity of Heaven, Earth, and man, without
realizing that the king is considered here as
representative of men. Moreover, in chapters 16
and 39, Heaven, Earth, and the king are spoken of
together.

5. Quoting Hsiao-ching[c] (Classic of filial
piety), chapter 9.

6. Compare Wang Pi, chapter 51.

7. Compare Wang Pi, chapter 4.

8. For the idea of two modes or molds, see
Wang Pi, chapter 4.

9. This passage from the second sentence on
is translated by Wing-tsit Chan and is quoted from
his A Source Book in Chinese Philosophy, pp. 321, 322.

CHAPTER 26

The heavy is the root of the light.

The tranquil is the ruler of the hasty.

> In general, things that are light cannot carry
> the heavy and things that are small cannot
> subdue the great. He who does not walk causes
> the walk. He who does not move controls the
> movement. Therefore the heavy is certainly the
> root of the light and the tranquil is certainly
> the master of the hasty.

Therefore the sage travels all day

Without leaving his baggage.

> He considers the heavy to be the root. There-
> fore (he) does not leave his baggage.

Even at the sight of magnificent scenes,

He remains leisurely and indifferent.

> He does not pay any attention.

How is it that a lord with ten thousand chariots

Should behave lightheartedly in his empire?

If he is lighthearted, the minister[1] will be

> destroyed.

If he is hasty, the ruler is lost.

> Being lighthearted means being unable to
> subdue the heavy. One loses the root because
> one loses the body. The master is lost because
> the position of ruler is lost.

NOTE

1. Chan's note (p. 146, note 4): The word "root," rather than "minister," appears in the Wang Pi and Ho-shang Kung and many other texts. Many texts have "minister," which rhymed with the word for ruler.

CHAPTER 27

A good traveler leaves no track or trace.

 If one acts according to Tzu-jan without

 creating or starting things, things will reach

 their goal and leave no track or trace.

A good speech leaves no flaws.

 If one follows the nature of things without

 separating or dividing, no flaws will reach

 one's door.

A good reckoner uses no counters.

 That means following the course of things

 without depending on forms.

A well-shut door needs no bolts, and yet it cannot

 be opened.

A well-tied knot needs no rope, and yet none can

 untie it.

 If one follows the natural state of things

 without establishing or exerting anything,

 then there is no need for bolts or ropes and

 yet no one can open or untie it. All these

 five speak of following the nature of things

 without creating or exerting and without

 restricting things by forms.[1]

Therefore the sage is always good in saving men and

 consequently no man is rejected.

 The sage does not institute forms and names

 to restrain things. He does not formulate

 standards of advance so that the degenerate will

83

be discarded. Instead, he assists all things

in their natural state but does not play the

part of their origin.[2] This is why it is

said that the sage never discards anyone. "Do

not exalt the worthy, so that the people shall

not compete. Do not value rare treasures, so

that the people shall not steal. Do not dis-

play objects of desire, so that the people's

hearts shall not be disturbed."[3] If people are

always enabled to free their minds from doubts

and desires, they will not be discarded.[4]

Consequently, no man is rejected.

He is always good in saying things and consequently

nothing is rejected.

This is called following[5] the light (of Nature).

Therefore the good man is the teacher of the bad.

(The sage) chooses the good to teach the bad.

Therefore he is said to be a teacher.

And the bad is the material from which the good

may learn.

Tzu[a] (material) means to choose or to take.

The good man saves the bad with the good and

also discards the bad with the good.

Therefore the bad ones are chosen by the

good ones.[6]

He who does not value the teacher.

Or greatly care for the material,

Is greatly deluded although he may be learned.

Although one has knowledge, if he relies on

it but does not follow things with Tao, he
certainly will be lost. Therefore it is said,
"He is greatly deluded although he may be
learned."

Such is the essential mystery.

NOTES

1. Compare similar statements in Wang Pi,
chapter 36.

2. Paraphrasing Lao Tzu, chapter 64.

3. Lao Tzu, chapter 3.

4. Paraphrasing Lao Tzu, chapter 3. The
translation of this extensive paragraph has been
adapted from Chan, A Source Book in Chinese
Philosophy, p. 322.

5. Chan's note (p. 148, note 3): The word
hsi[b], here rendered as "following," is open to
various interpretations: "To cover, "to penetrate,"
"to practice," "to secure by devious means,"
"double," and so forth. According to Ma Hsü-lun's
commentary on chapter 52, this hsi and the hsi[c]
meaning "practice" were interchangeable in ancient
times, but it is most often understood as
"following."

6. Read ch'i[d] (to equalize) as chi[e] (to save).
In any case, Wang Pi departs from the original
meaning of tzu as material in the Lao Tzu and
interpreted it to mean to take.

CHAPTER 28

He who knows the male and keeps to the female

Becomes the ravine of the world.

Being the ravine of the world,

He will never depart from eternal virtue,

But return to the state of infancy.

The male belongs to the first, the female

belongs to afterward. Knowing that if we want

to be the first in the world, we will certainly

have to be the last. "Therefore the sage

places himself in the background but finds

himself in the foreground."[1] The ravine

does not seek for things and yet things return

to it of themselves. An infant uses no

knowledge but harmonizes with the knowledge

of Tzu-jan.

He who knows the white and yet keeps to the black

Becomes the model of the world.

Model means to be the standard or pattern.

Being the model for the world,

He will never deviate from eternal virtue.

To deviate means to be mistaken.

But returns to the state of the Ultimate of Nonbeing.

This means to be inexhaustible.

He who knows glory but keeps to humanity

Becomes the valley of the world.

Being the valley of the world,

He will be proficient in eternal virtue,

And returns to the state of simplicity (uncarved wood).

These three[2] means always to return. Only when that is done can virtue be complete wherever one may be. In a later chapter it is said, "Reversion is the action of Tao."[3] Success cannot be seized, for one always remains with the Mother.

When the uncarved wood is broken up, it is turned into concrete things.[4]

But when the sage uses it, he becomes the leading official.

Uncarved wood means essence. When essence is scattered, its different dispositions produce multiplicity, and species come into being as concrete things. Because they are scattered, the sage institutes rules for them, let good be their teacher and evil be their material[5] [as object lessons], changes their way of life, and transforms their customs so they will return to the One.[6]

Therefore the great ruler does not cut up.

He who rules greatly takes the art of the world as his own. Therefore he does not cut up.

NOTES

1. Quoting Lao Tzu, chapter 7.

2. Returning to the state of infancy. Ultimate of Nonbeing, and simplicity, according to Den Shiryū.

3. Quoting Lao Tzu, chapter 40.

4. Chan's note (p. 150, note 3): As Tao is transformed into the myriad things. The word ch'i[a], translated as "utensils" in chapter 11, should be understood here in its more general sense of concrete things. In later philosophy, especially in Neo-Confucianism, ch'i is contrasted with Tao, which has neither physical restriction nor physical form, but its meaning is not as general as matter, substance, or material entity.

5. Paraphrasing Wang Pi, chapter 27.

6. Translation of this paragraph is by Chan, A Source Book in Chinese Philosophy, p. 322.

CHAPTER 29

When one desires to take over the empire and act

    on it (interfere with it),

I see that he will not succeed.

The empire is a spiritual thing, and should not

    be acted on.

    Spirit has no physical form and has no spatial

    restriction, whereas concrete things (ch'i[a])

    are produced through an integration of elements.

    When there is an integration without form, it

    is therefore called a spiritual thing.[1]

He who acts on it harms it.

He who holds on to it loses it.

    The nature of the myriad things in spontaneity.

    It should be followed but not interfered with.[2]

    One can penetrate this nature, but one cannot

    rigidly hold on to it. Things have an eternal

    nature, and if we artificially interfere with

    it, we shall surely fail. Things come into

    and go out of being, and if we would hold on to

    them, we certainly lose them.

Among creatures some lead and some follow.

Some blow hot and some blow cold.

Some are strong and some are weak.

Some may break and some may fall.

Therefore the sage discards the extremes, the extra-

vagant, and the excessive.

    All these examples show that all things and

all affairs, whether in their favorable or
unfavorable circumstances, and whether in their
forward or backward movements, are not to be
interfered with through action or held onto.
The sage understands the nature of <u>Tzu-jan</u>[3]
perfectly and knows clearly the conditions of
all things. Therefore he goes along with them
but takes no unnatural action. He is in harmony
with them but does not impose anything on them.
He removes their delusions and eliminates their
doubts. Hence the people's minds are not
confused and things are contented with their
own nature.[4]

NOTES

1. Translation of this paragraph is by Chan,
<u>A Source Book in Chinese Philosophy</u>, p. 322.

2. The translation of this sentence is taken
from Chan, ibid.

3. According to T'ao Hung-ch'ing, the word
<u>chih</u>[b] (to arrive) should be <u>hsing</u>[c] (nature). He
is correct because it agrees with the earlier
sentence, "The nature of the myriad things spontaneity." We may add that "nature" also parallels
<u>ch'ing</u>[d] (conditions) in the clause that immediately
follows here.

4. Translation beginning with "The sage
understands" is by Chan, ibid.

CHAPTER 30

He who assists the ruler with Tao does not dominate

the world with force.

Even one who assists the ruler with Tao may

not dominate the empire with force of arms.

How much less may the ruler who practices Tao!

The use of force usually brings requital.

A ruler[1] insists on piling up accomplishments

and starting activities, but he who practices

Tao devotes himself entirely to returning (to

the root) and taking no action. Therefore it

is said that a thing naturally brings a return.

Wherever armies are stationed, briers and thorns grow.

Great wars are always followed by famines.

This means that an army portends evil and injury.

If there is nothing which helps, there will

certainly be injury to others in plundering and

wounding people and destroying the fields.

Therefore it is said, "Briers and thorns grow."

A good (general)[2] achieves his purpose and stops,

But dares not seek to dominate the world.

To achieve purposes means to help. This is to

say that he who knows how to employ an army aims

only at saving people from disaster, and that

is all. His purpose is not to dominate the

world by force of arms.

He achieves his purpose but does not bring about it.

He achieves his purpose but does not boast about it.

He achieves his purpose but is not proud of it.

I do not consider the Tao of the army as
something to be honored, but if I have no choice
but to use it, what is there to brag about
or to be .proud of?

He achieves his purpose but only as an unavoidable
step.

He achieves his purpose but does not aim to dominate.

This is to say that if he uses force, although
he aims at success and his objective is to
save people from disaster, yet only in times
when this is an unavoidable step that one
should employ it to abolish terror and disorder but should not aim at domination.

(For) after things reach their prime, they begin
to grow old,

Which means being contrary to Tao.

Whatever is contrary to Tao will soon perish.

Reaching the prime state means a sudden rise
in military power. It illustrates those who
dominate the world by force. "A whirlwind
does not last a whole morning. Nor does a
rainstorm last a whole day."[3] Therefore
a sudden rise is contrary to Tao and will
soon perish.

NOTES

1. In the <u>Tao-te chen-ching chi-chu</u>, <u>shih</u>[a] (beginning) is <u>chih</u>[b] (to rule).

2. Chan's note (p. 152, note 2): The <u>che</u>[c] (person, he who) in the Ho-shang Kung and fifty-three other texts makes better sense than the <u>yu</u>[d] (to have) in the Wang Pi text.

3. Quoting <u>Lao Tzu</u>, chapter 23.

CHAPTER 31

Fine weapons are instruments of evil.

They are hated by men.

Therefore those who possess Tao turn away from them.

The good ruler when at home honors the left.

When at war he honors the right.

Weapons are instruments of evil, not the instruments
of a good ruler.

When he uses them unavoidably, he regards calm
restraint as the best principle.

Even when he is victorious, he does not regard it
as praiseworthy,

For to praise victory is to delight in the slaughter
of men.

He who delights in the slaughter of men will not
succeed in the empire.

In auspicious affairs, the left is honored.

In inauspicious affairs, the right is honored.

The lieutenant general stands on the left.

The senior general stands on the right.

This is to say that the arrangement follows that
of funeral ceremonies.[1]

For a slaughter of the multitude, let us weep with
sorrow and grief.

For a victory, let us observe the occasion with
the funeral ceremonies.

[The present Wang Pi commentary contains no
comments on this chapter and chapter 66.][2]

NOTES

1. Chan's note (p. 155, note 6): Most commentators agree that these last twelve lines, if not the entire chapter, are a mixture of commentary and text. The sixth line, particularly, sounds like a commentary on the first line. These last five sentences interrupt the preceding and following passages. They contain the terms "lieutenant general" and "senior general", which did not appear until Han times (B.C. 206-220 A.D.). Moreover, this chapter and chapter 66 are the only two in the present Wang Pi text which contain no comments. These five sentences may possibly have been his commentary, although his commentaries in other chapters are more philosophical and more plentiful. But both Tung Ssu-ching and Chao Ping-wen say Wang added a note to this chapter, saying, "I suspect it was not written by Lao Tzu." This note is not found in the present text but still appears in a manuscript (A.D. 1235) in Japan. Kanō Naoki saw this note in the Bibliothèque Nationale at Paris, in a fragment discovered in a Tun-huang[a] cave. See his Chūgoku tetsugaku shi (History of Chinese philosophy), p. 181. It may be an explanation of Wang's failure to comment on this chapter.

2. In the Tao-te chen-ching chi-chu, Wang Pi is quoted as saying, "I suspect that this was not written by Lao Tzu." See Hatano, II, pp. 59-62,

for a full discussion on this matter. Liu Kuo-chün has noted that the notation attributed to Wang Pi does not appear in the Taoist Canon edition of his commentary but argues that Wang Pi must have seen Lao Tzu 31 and did not believe it was by Lao Tzu.

CHAPTER 32

Tao is eternal and has no name.

Though its simplicity seems insignificant, none in
the world can master it.

If kings and barons would hold on to it, all things
would submit to them spontaneously.

Tao has neither form nor restriction (attachment).[1] Being eternal, it cannot be named.
Its eternity consists in namelessness. We can
never name it. That it is nameless gives it
permanence. Therefore it is said, "Tao is
eternal and has no name." That which is called
simplicity, its heart (essence) is nothingness,
and it also has no name. Therefore to reach
Tao, there is nothing better than maintaining
simplicity. He who is wise can serve with
ability. He who is courageous can perform
duties with bravery. He who is skillful can
handle affairs. He who is strong can assume
heavy responsibility. That which is known as
simplicity is at ease and is not partial. It
is almost like having nothing. Therefore it is
said, "None in the world can master it." If
someone embraces simplicity and takes no action,
does not impede his true nature with material
things, and does not harm his spirit with desires,
things will submit to him spontaneously and Tao
can be attained of itself.

Heaven and earth unite to drip sweet dew.

Without the command of men, it drips evenly over all.

This means that if heaven and earth unite, then sweet dew will fall of itself without being sought. If I adhere to its true nature and take no action, then without my command, people will naturally become well adjusted.

As soon as there were regulations and institutions, there were names.

As soon as there are names, know that it is time to stop.

It is by knowing when to stop that one can be free from danger.

"As soon as there were regulations and institutions" means that simplicity has disappeared.[2] It is the time when officials were first appointed. When there are institutions and officials, there must be ranks and titles to determine the upper and lower grades. Therefore "As there were regulations and institutions, there are names." From then on, any dispute will be concerned with small details. Therefore it is said, "As soon as there are names, know that it is time to stop." When thereafter everything is docketed, one loses the mother of government. Therefore, "It is by knowing when to stop that one can be free from danger."

Analogically, Tao in the world may be compared to rivers and streams running into the sea.

When rivers and streams seek the sea, it is
not the sea which calls for them. Without being
called or asked, they return naturally. As Tao
operates in the world, it is naturally even
without anyone commanding it, and it is achieved
without seeking. Therefore it is said, "Tao may
be compared to rivers and streams running into
the sea."

NOTES

1. For these descriptions, see Wang
Pi, chapter 21.

2. The expression p'u-san[a] (simplicity
disappears) also appears in Lao Tzu, chapter
28: "When the uncarved wood (simplicity) is
broken up...."

CHAPTER 33

He who knows others is wise;

He who knows himself is enlightened.

> He who knows others is merely wise. It is not
> as good as knowing oneself, which surpasses
> wisdom.

He who conquers others has physical strength.

He who conquers himself is strong.

> He who conquers others merely has physical
> strength. It is not as good as he who conquers
> himself; nothing can impair his strength. To
> apply one's knowledge to others is not as good
> as to apply this knowledge to oneself. Applying
> one's strength to others is not as good as
> applying it to oneself. If one applies such
> knowledge to oneself, then things cannot hide
> from him. If one applies this strength to
> oneself, then things cannot attack him.[1]

He who is contented is rich.

> He who is contented naturally will not lose.
> Therefore he is rich.

He who acts with vigor has will.

> He who pursues his purpose diligently will
> certainly attain his goal. Therefore it is
> said, "He who acts with vigor has will."

He who does not lose his place (with Tao) will endure.

> If one examines oneself intelligently, acts
> in accordance with one's own capacity,

and does not lose one's place (with Tao),

one will certainly endure.

He who dies but does not really perish enjoys

long life.

Though one dies, the Tao of life does not

perish, and one completes one's long life.

The body perishes but Tao still remains.

All the more if the body persists and Tao

will not perish.

NOTE

1. According to Hattori Nankaku, kai[a]
(to change) should read kung[b] (to attack). See
Hatano, II, p. 74. Yen Ling-feng agrees.

CHAPTER 34

The Great Tao flows everywhere.

It may go left or right.

> This means that Tao overflows and goes every-
> where. It can be on the right or on the left,
> above or below. It operates all around.
> Therefore there is no place where it does not
> reach.

All things depend on it for life, and it does not
turn away from them.

It accomplishes its task, but does not claim credit
for it.

It clothes and feeds all things but does not claim
to be master over them.

Always without desires, it may be called The Small.

> The myriad things all come from Tao. When they
> are born, they know not whence they come.
> Therefore if in the world one remains without
> desires, then each of the myriad things comes
> to the right place. If Tao does not act, then
> we call it The Small.

All things come to it and it does not master them;
it may be called The Great.

> The myriad things all return to Tao in order
> to live and[1] [Tao] causes the myriad things to
> ignore their source. From this point of view,
> it is not The Small. Therefore we also may call
> it The Great.

Therefore (the sage) never strives himself for the great, and thereby the great is achieved.

"Prepare for the difficult while it is easy. Deal with the big while it is still small."[2]

NOTES

1. Scholars like Tsukada Taihō and Yen Ling-feng agree that the word li^a (strength) here is superfluous.

2. Quoting Lao Tzu, chapter 63.

CHAPTER 35

Hold fast to that great form (Tao),

And all the world will come.

The great form is the mother of the heavenly

images. It is neither hot[1] nor cold, neither

warm nor cool. Therefore it can embrace the

myriad things and there is nothing which it

would harm. If the master holds to this, then

all the world will come.

They come and will encounter no harm;

But enjoy comfort, peace, and health.

Without form, without knowledge, without

partiality, without being evident,[2] therefore

the myriad things come to it and encounter no

harm.

When there are music and dainties,

Passing strangers will stay.

But the words uttered by Tao,

How insipid and tasteless!

We look at it; it is imperceptible.

We listen to it; it is inaudible.

We use it; it is inexhaustible.

These words describe the depth and the greatness

of Tao. A human being hears the words of Tao,

but they are not like music or dainties. The

human heart corresponds to the times and feels

happy. Joy and dainties can induce "passing

strangers to stay, but the words uttered by Tao,

how insipid and tasteless!" If we look at it,
it is imperceptible and not enough to delight
the eyes. If we listen to it, it is inaudible
and not enough to rejoice the ears. It is as if
Tao had no objective. But if we use it, it can
never be exhausted.

NOTES

1. Add pu-yen[a] (not hot) here, according to
Yen Ling-feng. T'ao Hung-ch'ing had suggested that
pu-yen be added at the end, in this order: cold -
warm - hot - cool. The order seems logical because
cold-warm and hot-cool are parallel. However, Yen's
order, hot-cold warm-cool, is also parallel. Besides,
Yen has the support of Wang Pi's other writings where
the sequence of warm-cool and hot-cold are used. In
Wang Pi, chapter 41, the sequence is warm-hot, hot-
cold.

2. The same phrase appears in Wang Pi,
chapter 16.

CHAPTER 36

In order to contract,

It is necessary first to expand.

In order to weaken,

It is necessary first to strengthen.

In order to destroy,

It is necessary first to promote.

In order to grasp,

It is necessary first to give.

This is called subtle light.

If one wishes to remove violent and fierce[1] people, in the case of these four things, one should follow the nature of things and let them destroy themselves. One should not trust punishment as great in order to remove things.[2] Therefore it is called subtle light. If one lets them expand sufficiently and one even further expands them, then everything will contract. If one helps those who have not sufficiently expanded and then demand them to expand further and further, one will instead encounter danger oneself.[3]

The weak and the tender overcome the hard and the strong.

Fish should not be taken away from water.

And sharp weapons of the state should not be displayed to the people.

Sharp weapons mean implements, which are of

benefit[4] to the country. Only by following
the nature of things, without resorting to
punishment,[5] can things be managed. But if by
the imperceptible implement everything finds
its own place, then that is the sharp weapon
for the state. He who demonstrates this to
others relies on punishment. If one relies on
punishment to benefit a country, that will be
a mistake. If a fish is removed from the
depths, it will certainly be shown to be a
mistake. If to benefit a state one institutes
punishment in order to demonstrate to the
people, that will be a mistake too.

NOTES

1. Compare Lao Tzu, chapter 42: "Violent
and fierce people do not die a natural death."

2. The text here is corrupted but the sense
is clear.

3. The text here is obscure.

4. Li[a] means both sharp and benefit.

5. Compare a similar statement in Wang Pi,
chapters 23, 41.

CHAPTER 37

Tao invariably takes no action,

    This means to follow Nature.[1]

  and yet there is nothing left undone.

    The myriad things follow it to begin[2] and

    complete its being.

If kings and barons can keep it, all things will

    transform spontaneously.

If, after transformation, they should desire to

    be active,

I would restrain them with simplicity, which has·

    no name.

    "If after transformation they should desire

    to be active" means that the desire to be

    active is realized. "I would restrain them

    with simplicity, which has no name" means that

    I will not be their master.

Simplicity, which has no name, is free of desires.

    This means that there is no desire to complete.[3]

Being free of desires, it is tranquil.

And the world will be at peace of its own accord.

NOTES

    1. Compare a similar statement in Wang Pi,
chapter 25.

    2. Read chih[a] (to rule) as shih[b] (to begin),
according to a number of writers. See Hatano,
II, p. 92, T'ao Hung-ch'ing, and Yen Ling-feng.

    3. Wang Pi's sentence is probably incomplete.

CHAPTER 38

The man of superior virtue is not (conscious of)
    his virtue,

And in this way he really possesses virtue.

The man of inferior virtue never loses (sight of)
    his virtue,

And in this way he loses his virtue.

The man of superior virtue takes no action, but
    has no ulterior motive to do so.

The man of inferior virtue takes action, and has an
    ulterior motive to do so.

The man of superior humanity takes action, but has
    no ulterior motive to do so.

The man of superior righteousness takes action,
    and has an ulterior motive to do so.

The man of superior propriety[1] takes action,

And when people do not respond to it, he will
    stretch his arms and force it on them.

Therefore when Tao is lost, only then does the
    doctrine of virtue arise.

When virtue is lost, only then does the doctrine of
    humanity arise.

When humanity is lost, only then does the doctrine
    of righteousness arise.

When righteousness is lost, only then does the
    doctrine of propriety arise.

Now, propriety is a superficial expression of
    loyalty and faithfulness, and the beginning

Those who are the first to know have the flowers of

Tao but are the beginning of ignorance.

For this reason the great man dwells in the thick,

and does not rest with the thin.

He dwells in the fruit, and does not rest with the

flower.

Therefore he rejects the one, and accepts the other.

Te[a] (virtue) means te[b] (to attain). It is

constant attainment without loss and benefit

without harm. Therefore we call it te. How

is virtue to be attained? It is to be attained

through Tao. How is virtue to be completely

fulfilled? It is through nonbeing as its

function. As nonbeing is its function, all

things will be embraced. Therefore in regard

to things, if they are understood as nonbeing,

all things will be in order, whereas if they

are understood as being, it is impossible to

avoid the fact that they are products (phenom-

ena). Although Heaven and Earth are extensive,

nonbeing is the mind, and although sages and

kings are great, vacuity is their foundation.

Therefore it is said that if we see things by

their return,[2] the mind of Heaven and Earth will

be revealed.[3] If one thinks of the solstice,

then one sees the ultimate of former kings.[4]

Therefore if one destroys oneself and one's ego,

then all people within the four seas will respect

him and will come to him from far and near.

If one considers oneself to be something special
and sets one's heart on something, then one's
body cannot be preserved, and one's muscles and
bones cannot tolerate each other.

Therefore the man of superior virtue makes use
only of Tao. He will not consider his virtue
as a virtue. He will not hold on to anything
or use anything. Therefore he has virtue and
can accomplish anything. He does not strive
but accomplishes everything.[5] Therefore
although he does indeed have virtue, he does not
possess the nature of virtue.

The man of inferior virtue strives and
achieves; he acts and accomplishes. Thus he
must establish the good in order to be able to
manage things. Therefore he has the name of
virtue. If one strives for success, one will
certainly lose sometimes. If one acts to
perfect things, one will certainly fail sometimes. Where the name of good arises, there
will be evil to correspond to it. Therefore
"A man of inferior virtue takes action and has
an ulterior motive to do so or acts intention-
ally." Not to act for ulterior motives means
not to act onesidedly. All those who cannot
refrain from action but must act are of inferior
virtue. Humanity, righteousness, ceremonies,
and regulations are such.

To make clear whether virtue is superior or inferior one always contrasts superior virtue with inferior virtue until the point of having no ulterior motive is reached. The ultimate capacity of inferior virtue is superior humanity. When superior humanity develops to the point where there are no ulterior motives and yet one still acts and yet acts in such a way as to have no ulterior motives, one thus has the trouble of doing something. The roots lie in taking no action and the Mother is the unnamed. If by abandoning the roots and discarding the Mother one goes to the son (the nonessential), then although one's accomplishment is great, certainly there will be failure, and although one's name is beautiful, falsehood will certainly arise. If one cannot accomplish without action and manage without stirring up things and goes on to act, one will love people with extensive and universal benevolence and love without partiality or selfishness. Such is therefore the case where "Superior humanity takes action but has no ulterior motive to do so." When love cannot be universal, there will be those who resist that which is correct and upright.[6] Those who apply righteousness to straighten out matters will rage against injustice and protect uprightness, or help this and attack that. Thus things will be done with intent. Therefore "Superior righteousness takes action but has an ulterior motive to do so."

If justice is not earnest, then there are superficial embellishments. Those who pay homage to and revere such embellishments will like to cultivate reverence. They will be exacting and demanding in dealing with others. Whenever there is anything wrong, they will get angry. Therefore, "The man of superior propriety takes action, and when people do not respond to it, he will stretch his arms and force it on them."

Tao is indeed the ultimate of greatness. Anything beyond it is not worth honoring. Although [Heaven and Earth] are engaged in great understandings and have great wealth[7] in possessing the myriad things, each thing still has its own character. Although it is valuable to have nonbeing as its function, nevertheless there cannot be substance without nonbeing.[8] If there cannot be substance without nonbeing, then what makes it great is lost. This is why it is said, "When Tao is lost, only then does the doctrine of virtue arise."

If one takes nonbeing as function, one obtains the Mother, and therefore one does not labor hard and all things are in order. Beyond this, one will lose the Mother of function. If one

cannot refrain from action, one will highly
honor universal benevolence. If one cannot
practice universal benevolence, one will highly
honor correctness and uprightness. If one cannot
pursue correctness and uprightness, one will
highly honor embellishments and reverence. That
is why it is said, "When virtue is lost, only
then does the doctrine of humanity arise. When
humanity is lost, only then does the doctrine
of righteousness arise. When righteousness is
lost, only then does the doctrine of propriety
arise."
Now propriety arises first of all from superficial loyalty and faithfulness and lack of
openness,[9] the stress on appearance, and the
struggle to control trivialities. Righteousness and propriety issue from within, but if
one practices them, they are still artificial.
How long can they last if one engages in
external decorum? Therefore "Propriety[10] is a
superficial expression of loyalty and faithfulness and is the beginning of disorder."
Those who are first to know are those who
try to know before others do. They belong to
the group of inferior virtue. They exhaust
their intelligence in order to know first and
apply their intellectual power to operate various
things. Although their hearts are genuine,
they are treacherous and clever and all the more

subtle. Although their praise is ample, all the more their earnestness is lost. They labor, but their work becomes obscure, and they work, but their management is spoiled. Though they exhaust their wisdom, yet people are still more harmed.

If one abandons oneself and leaves things alone,[11] then without taking action, there will be peace. If one keeps to simplicity, then one does not follow tradition an institutions. One acquiesces in what this person receives but rejects what that person holds onto. "Those who are the first[12] to know have the flowers of Tao but are the beginning of ignorance." Therefore if one obtains the Mother of how to make effort, then "All things arise, and he does not turn away from them,"[13] and all things are supported and preserved and not troubled. When one functions without physical form and commands without name, humanity and righteousness will be manifest and propriety and reverence will become prominent.

When things are supported by the great Tao and guarded by the nameless, then things are not glorified and the mind does not calculate. If everyone realizes his reality (truth) and all things are done with sincerity, then human virtue is rich, the principle of conduct is correct, and propriety and reverence become pure.

If one rejected what is supported and discards
what is produced, if people make use of their
completed form and employ their intelligence
like a slave, then humanity becomes falsehood,[14]
righteousness becomes competition, and propriety
becomes struggle. Therefore the richness of
the virtue of humanity cannot be (obtained)
through utilizing humanity, the correctness of
the principle of conduct cannot be realized by
utilizing righteousness, and the purity of
propriety and reverence cannot be accomplished
by utilizing ceremony.

Support things with Tao, and command and unite
them with the Mother. Therefore one should
manifest them without glorifying them, and make
them prominent without any ambition. One uses
the nameless and the name is thereby real. One
uses the formless and the form is thereby
completed. When one holds on to the Mother to
preserve the son, and honors the roots in order
to promote the branches, there will be both
physical form and name and evil will not arise.
The great beauty will match Heaven and flowers
will not grow. Therefore the Mother should not
be discarded and the roots should not be lost.
Humanity and righteousness are produced by the
Mother, but they cannot be the Mother. Forms
and things were made by artisans, but they
cannot be artisans. If one discards one's Mother

and uses her son, and if one discards the roots and goes towards the branches, then names will bring on division and things and shape will impose a limit. Although the greatness is of the highest degree, there will surely be something not included, and although the praise is very extensive, there will surely be trouble. If the effort is to take action, is that something one should abide in?

NOTES

1. Chan's note (p. 169, note 3): In a narrow sense, $\underline{li}^c$ (propriety) means rites, ritual, ceremonies, etc., but in a broad sense it means rules of behavior or principles of conduct.

2. Referring to Lao Tzu, chapter 16.

3. The passage beginning with "how is virtue" up to this point has been adapted from Chan, Source Book, p. 322.

4. Wang Pi is here paraphrasing the Book of Changes, hexagram no. 24, $\underline{Fu}^d$ (to return). Mou Tsung-san, in his Ts'ai-hsing yü hsüan-li (Capacity, nature, and metaphysic), p. 165, suggests amending $\underline{chih}^e$ (ultimate) with $\underline{chih}^f$ (intention), making the sentence to read, "We can see the intentions of former kings." However, in the Book of Changes, solstice refers to the ultimate point where the process of returning starts.

5. Compare Lao Tzu, ch. 47.

6. The Tao-te chen-ching chi-chu and other texts have chih[g] (upright) instead of chen[h] (true). See Yen Ling-feng.

7. Paraphrasing the Book of Changes, "Appended Remarks," Part I, chapter 5. Following this sentence, some editions have the following, which makes no sense: And cannot achieve self-completion. Therefore heaven cannot carry, earth cannot cover, and man cannot support.

8. The translation of this paragraph up to this point has been taken from Chan, A Source Book in Chinese Philosophy, p. 323. Mou Tsung-san (p. 166) thinks that she[i] (to discard), here translated as "without," should read chü[j] (to dwell in), meaning, "One should not dwell in or hold on to non being as substance," Ch'ien Mu, however, interprets the sentence to mean that non being as function should be discarded, for non being is substance. See his Chung-kuo ssu-hsiang shih (History of Chinese thought), p. 94.

9. In the Tao-te chen-ching chi-chu, yang[k] (bright) reads ch'ang[l] (clear and free).

10. Liu Kuo-chün has observed that the Taoist Canon edition has shih-li[m] (loss of propriety) instead of fu li[n] (now, propriety) and remarks that if this is correct and if Wang Pi had followed the Lao Tzu text, it would mean that Lao Tzu was defending

118

propriety rather than attacking it. Liu concedes, however, that there is not enough evidence to support this contention.

11. See a similar statement in Wang Pi, chapter 5.

12. According to Tōjō Ichitō, Hattori Nankaku, et al., agree that the word ch'ien[o] (first) should be added here. See Hatano, II, p. 115.

13. Quoting Lao Tzu, chapter 2.

14. Hattori Nankaku, Usami Shinsui, Tsukada Taihō, Tōjō Ichitō, et al., all read ch'eng[p] (sincerity) as wei[q] (insincerity, false). See Hatano, II, pp. 116-117.

CHAPTER 39

Of old those that obtained the One:

> "Of old" means in the beginning. One is the
> beginning of number and the ultimate of things.
> All things are produced by the One and this is
> why it is the master of all. And all things
> achieve their completion because of the One.[1]
> However, as soon as completed, they leave this
> One[2] to hold on to their completion. In thus
> holding on to their completion, they lose their
> Mother. Therefore they crack, they are shaken,
> they wither away, become exhausted, become
> extinct, and fall.

Heaven obtained the One and became clear.

Earth obtained the One and became tranquil.

The spiritual beings obtained the One and became
divine.

The valley obtained the One and became full.

The myriad things obtained the One and lived and grew.

Kings and barons obtained the One and became rulers
of the empire.

What made them so is the One.[3]

> Through this One, each of these becomes clear,
> tranquil, divine, full, growing, and rulers.

If heaven had not thus become clear,

It would soon crack.

> With the One, it achieves clearness, but it
> achieves clearness not by clearness. If it

adheres to the One, then clearness will not be
lost. If it uses clearness, it will probably
crack. Therefore the Mother of the results
cannot be discarded. For this reason, heaven,
and so on, would not use their results, fearing
thereby to lose their roots.

If the earth had not thus become tranquil,

It would soon be shaken.

If the spiritual beings had not thus become divine,

They would soon wither away.

If the valley had not thus become full,

It would soon become exhausted.

If the myriad things had not thus lived and grown,

They would soon become extinct.

If kings and barons had not thus become honorable
and high in position,

They would soon fall.

Therefore humble station is the basis of honor.

The low is the foundation of the high.

For this reason kings and barons call themselves
children without parents, lonely people without
spouses, and men without food to eat.

Is this not regarding humble station as the basis
of honor?

Is it not?

Therefore enumerate all the parts of a chariot as
you may, and you still have no chariot.[4]

Rather than jingle like the jade,

Rumble like the rocks.

Clearness cannot create clearness, and
fullness cannot create fullness. Everything
has its Mother so as to preserve its form
(shape). Therefore clearness is not greatly
honored and fullness is not highly valued.
What is honorable lies with the Mother, and
the Mother honors the formless. "Humble
station is the basis of honor (and) the low
is the foundation of the high....Therefore to
attain fame repeatedly is no fame.[5] Jade and
stones jingle and rumble. Their substance
all lies in their form. Therefore one should
not desire it.[6]

NOTES

1. The last three sentences have been translated by Chan, Source Book, p. 323.

2. The "one" here is added according to the Tao-te chen-ching chi-chu.

3. Chan's note (p. 171, note 2): Neither the Wang Pi nor the Ho Shang-kung text has the word "One," but the Fu I and twenty-four other texts have it, according to Chiang Hsi-ch'ang.

4. Chan's note (p. 171, note 5): The Wu Ch'eng text reads: "Therefore supreme praise is no praise."

5. Both the Lao Tzu text and the Wang Pi commentary read literally, "Therefore enumerate all the parts of a chariot as you may, and you still have no chariot." Some editions have chih[a] (supreme) instead of chih[b] (to attain) and many editions have yü[c] (fame) instead of yü[d] (chariot). Here to read yü as fame agrees better with the preceding sentences, as most writers have maintained. See Hatano, II, pp. 125-126.

6. Unlike other commentators like Ho-shang Kung, who interpreted jade as high and stone as low, with lowliness preferred, Wang Pi interpreted Lao Tzu's sentence as meaning that both jade and stone are undesirable.

CHAPTER 40

Reversion is the action of Tao.

"The low is the foundation of the high; humble station is the basis of honor."[1] Nonbeing is the function of being.[2] This is its reversion. However we act, if we know that there is nonbeing, all things will interpenetrate. Therefore it is said, "Reversion is the action of Tao."

Weakness is the function of Tao.

Weakness and gentleness interpenetrate and cannot be exhausted.

All things in the world come from being.

And being comes from nonbeing.

All things in the world came from being, and the origin of being is based on nonbeing. To have being in total, it is necessary to return to nonbeing.[3]

NOTES

1. Quoting <u>Lao Tzu</u>, chapter 39.

2. Compare <u>Lao Tzu</u>, chapter 11.

3. This translation is taken from Chan, <u>Source Book</u>, p. 323.

CHAPTER 41

When the highest type of men hear Tao,

They diligently practice it.

Because they have the will to do so.

When the average type of men hear Tao,

They half believe in it.

When the lowest type of men hear Tao,

They laugh heartily at it.

If they did not laugh at it, it would not be Tao.

Therefore there is the established saying:

To establish means to construct, to set up.

The Tao which is bright appears to be dark.

"The sage is bright as light but does not
dazzle."[1]

The Tao which goes forward appears to fall backward.

"The sage places himself in the background,
but finds himself in the foreground. He puts
himself away, and yet he always remains."[2]

The Tao which is level appears uneven.

Being even means deep. The Tao of great levels
follows the nature of things. It does not keep
to its own evenness to divide things. Its
evenness is not seen, but, on the contrary,
it seems to be uneven.

Great virtue appears like a valley (hollow).

He will not consider his virtue as a virtue,
for he does not think of it.

Great purity appears like disgrace.

"He who knows the white and yet keeps to the black."[3] Great purity will then be achieved.

Far-reaching virtue appears as if insufficient.

Far-reaching virtue is not filled; it is empty, without form, and cannot be filled.

Solid virtue appears as if unsteady.

Being unsteady means to be a companion.[4] He who establishes virtue leaves things in their natural state, neither establishes nor bestows, and therefore seems to be a companion.[5]

True substance appears to be changeable.

He whose substance is true (genuine) is not proud of its genuineness (authenticity).

Therefore it is changeable.

The great square has no corners.

"(The sage) is as pointed as a square but does not pierce."[6] Therefore it has no corners.

The great implement (or talent) is slow to finish (or mature).

The great implement finishes (completes) the world without holding on to the whole or its parts. Therefore it must be slow to finish.

Great music sounds faint.

"We listen to it and do not hear it; its name is The Inaudible."[7] That means that (great) music cannot be heard. Where there is sound, there are parts or lots. If there are parts or lots, then there would not be the note of kung[a] (the fundamental note) but the note of shang[b]

(secondary note). If one begins to distinguish
or to divide, one cannot control the whole.
Therefore that which has sound is not great
music.

Great form has no shape.

If there is shape, then there are parts or lots.
Where there parts or lots, if it is not warm,
then it is hot, and if it is not hot, then it is
cold. Therefore if a form has shape, it is not
the great form.

Tao is hidden and nameless.

Yet it is Tao alone that skillfully provides for all
and brings them to perfection.

In general, all skillfulness is perfected through
Tao. In regard to forms, it is great form, but
the great form has no shape. In regard to music,
it is great music, but great music sounds faint.
Things are accomplished by Tao, but one does not
see their complete shape.[8] Therefore it is hidden and without name. To provide for others is
not only to supply them with what they need.
Once one provides others (with the One), it will
be sufficient to complete their virtue forever.
Therefore it is said to skillfully provide. To
bring things to completion, not in the way the
artisan cuts his object, but to enable all things
to attain their shape, is therefore said to be
skillful in perfecting.

NOTES

1. Quoting <u>Lao Tzu</u>, chapter 58.

2. Quoting <u>Lao Tzu</u>, chapter 7.

3. Quoting <u>Lao Tzu</u>, chapter 28.

4. The meaning here is very obscure.

5. None of the commentators has found a satisfactory emendation or a satisfactory interpretation.

6. Quoting <u>Lao Tzu</u>, chapter 58.

7. Quoting <u>Lao Tzu</u>, chapter 14.

8. A similar sentence appears in Wang Pi, chapter 6.

CHAPTER 42

Tao produced the One.

The One produced the two.

The two produced the three.

And the three produced the ten thousand things.

The ten thousand things carry the yin and embrace the
yang, and through the blending of the material
force[1] they achieve harmony.

People hate to be children without parents, lonely
people without spouses, or men without food
to eat.

And yet kings and lords call themselves by these
names.

Therefore it is often the case that things gain by
losing and lose by gaining.

The ten thousand things have ten thousand different forms, but in the final analysis they are
one. How did they become one? Because of nonbeing.[2] Through nonbeing, one reaches oneness.
This One may be called nonbeing. Since it is
already called One, how can there be no speech?
If there is speech and there is the One, is that
not two? If there is One, there are two, and
consequently three is produced. From nonbeing
to being, numbers come to an end here. Beyond
this, it does not belong to the current (way) of
Tao.[3] Therefore in the production of the myriad
things, I know its master. Although things exist

in ten thousand different forms, their material

forces are blended as one. The multitude have

their own minds, and different countries have

different customs. But if the one is attained,

there will be kings and dukes as their masters.

One is the master. How can it be abandoned?

The greater the number, the further we go astray.

We are nearer to [truth] if the number is re-

duced. When it is reduced to the least (one),

we shall arrive at the ultimate.[4] Even when one

has spoken of One, one will still arrive at

three. All the more if basically there is no

One, how then could one draw near to Tao? One

increases by diminishing. That is certainly not

empty speech.

What others have taught, I teach also:

I do not compel others to follow, but I follow

Nature and place ultimate principle in the fore-

front. If we follow it, there will be fortune,

and if we disobey it, there will be misfortune.[5]

Therefore if people teach each other to contra-

vene this, they will surely meet with misfortune.

This is the same as what I teach others not to

oppose it.

"Violent and fierce people do not die a natural

death."[6]

I shall make this the father[7] of my teaching.

"Violent and fierce people do not die a natural

death." When people teach each other to behave

violently, they do not[8] resemble my teaching that they should not be violent. To point out that violent and fierce people do not die a natural death is almost like saying that my teaching will bring good fortune. Therefore if we find people violating this teaching, they can conveniently be made the father.

NOTES

1. Ch'i[a], material force, vital force, matter-energy.

2. The translation of these two sentences is taken from Chan, Source Book, p. 323.

3. Paraphrasing Chuang Tzu, chapter 2 (1:35a).

4. The translation from "Therefore in the production" up to this point is taken from Chan, ibid.

5. The translation of this sentence is taken from Chan, ibid.

6. Chan's note (p. 177, note 1): The same saying appears in the inscription on a metal statue in the imperial ancestral temple that Confucius visited. The story and the inscription appear in the Shuo-yüan[b] (Collection of discourses, compiled by Liu Hsiang,[c] 77-6 B.C.), 10:16b-17a. Commentators say the Lao Tzu quotes from the inscription, but both may have quoted from a common source.

8. Read pi[d] (surely) as fei[e] (do not), according to Yen Ling-feng.

CHAPTER 43

The softest things in the world overcome the hardest

    things in the world.

    Air passes through everything and water

    penetrates everywhere.[1]

Nonbeing penetrates that in which there is no space.

Through this I know the advantage of taking no action.

    The soft and empty nonbeing penetrates every-

    thing. Nonbeing is inexhaustible. The softest

    cannot be bent. Inferring from this, I there-

    fore know the advantage of taking no action.

Few in world can understand the teaching without

    words and the advantage of taking no action.

NOTE

1. The phrase <u>ch'u-yü</u>[a] (comes out of),

preceding "penetrates," is superfluous, according

to some scholars. See Hatano, II, p. 143.

CHAPTER 44

Which does one love more, fame or one's own life?

He who honors his name and loves superiority
will alienate himself from others.

Which is more valuable, one's own life or wealth?

He who is greedy for things and can never have
enough will have little for himself.

Which is worse, gain or loss?

Which is worse, to attain great benefit or to
lose oneself?

Therefore he who has lavish desires will spend
extravagantly.

He who hoards most will lose heavily.

He who has lavish desires will not share with
others. He who hoards most will not split with
others. He who seeks much will be attacked
by many and will be hated by others. Therefore
he will incur great expenditure and will lose
heavily.

He who is contented suffers no disgrace.

He who knows when to stop is free from danger.

Therefore he can long endure.

CHAPTER 45

What is most perfect seems to be incomplete;

But its utility is unimpaired.

It completes a thing wherever it may without

resulting in a particular form. Therefore it

seems to be incomplete.

What is most full seems to be empty;

But its usefulness is inexhaustible.

That which is most full is proficient.[1] It

provides anything that comes along without any

attachment. Therefore it seems to be empty.

What is most straight seems to be crooked.

Being straight with everything as it comes along,

one's straightness is confined to oneself.[2]

Therefore it seems to be crooked.

The greatest skill seems to be clumsy.

The greatest skill follows Tzu-jan so as to com-

plete things and does not create strange or

extraordinary cases. Therefore it seems to be

clumsy.

The greatest eloquence seems to stutter.

The greatest eloquence follows things in

speaking but he himself does not make things up.

Therefore he seems to stutter.

Hasty movement overcomes cold,

(But) tranquility overcomes heat.

By being greatly tranquil,

One is qualified to be the ruler of the world.

134

Only when a hasty movement is complete can cold be overcome, but tranquility conquers heat by taking no action. If one infers from this principle, then "Being greatly tranquil, one is qualified to be the ruler of the world." By being tranquil, one preserves the genuineness of things while hasty movement violates their nature.[3] Therefore only by tranquility will the greatest things mentioned above be attained.

NOTES

1. Ch'ung[a] (empty) is to be taken as ch'ung[b] (proficient).

2. Read i[c] (one) as chi[d] (self), according to Hattori Nankaku and Yen Ling-feng.

3. See a similar statement in Wang Pi, chapter 60.

CHAPTER 46

When Tao prevails in the world, galloping horses
   are turned back to fertilize (the fields with
   their dung.)[1]

   When Tao prevails, people know when to be
   contented and when to stop. Without seeking
   outside, each cultivates the internal only.
   Therefore galloping horses are turned back to
   fertilize the fields with their dung.

When Tao does not prevail in the world, war horses
   thrive in the suburbs.

   When people are greedy and never have enough,
   everyone does not cultivate the internal but
   seeks the external. Therefore war horses
   thrive in the suburbs.

There is no calamity greater than lavish desires.[2]

There is no greater guilt than discontentment.

And there is no greater disaster than greed.

He who is contented with contentment is always
   contented.

NOTES

1. Chan's note (p. 181, note 1): As quoted by Chu Hsi, the sentence has an additional word, "cart," thus meaning that the horses are used to draw manure carts (Chu Tzu yü-lei, 125:12a). But no one, not even his pupil who recorded the saying, knew on what textual authority he added the word. Probably Chu Hsi was paraphrasing, as many Chinese writers often do when they quote.

2. Chan's note (p. 181, note 4): This sentence does not appear in the Wang Pi text but appears in fifty-one other texts, including the Ho-shang Kung and Fu I texts.

CHAPTER 47

One may know the world without going out of doors.

One may see the Way of Heaven without looking

through the windows.

Events have a source and things have a master.[1]

There may be many roads but their destination

is the same, and there may be a hundred deli-

berations but the result is the same.[2] There

is a great constancy in Tao, and there is a

generality in principle. By holding on to the

Tao of old, we can master the present. Although

we live in the present age, we can know the

primeval beginning.[3] This is why one may know

[the world] without going out of doors or

looking through the windows.

The further one goes, the less one knows.

Nonbeing is inherent in the One. But when we

look for it in the multiplicity of things, it

is like Tao which can be looked for but not

seen, listened to but not heard, reached for

but not touched. If we know it, we do not need

to go out of doors. If we do not know it, the

further we go, the more beclouded we become.

Therefore the sage knows without going about,

Understands[4] without seeing,

If we know the general principle of things, we

can know through thinking even if we do not

138

travel. If we know the basis of things, even
if we do not see them, we can understand the
principle of right and wrong (which governs
them).[5]

And accomplishes without any action.

If one understands the nature of things, one
must follow it, and that is all.[6] Therefore,
although no action is taken, things are
accomplished.

NOTES

1. Compare Lao Tzu, chapter 70 and Wang Pi,
chapter 49.

2. Paraphrasing the Book of Changes,
"Appended Remarks," Part II, chapter 5.

3. Paraphrasing Lao Tzu, chapter 14.

4. Chan's note (p. 183, note 1): The word
ming[a] ordinarily means "name," but is interchangeable
with ming[b] meaning "to understand."

5. The translation of Wang Pi's commentary in
this chapter so far is adapted from Chan, Source
Book, pp. 323-324.

6. A similar expression is found in Wang Pi,
chapter 27.

CHAPTER 48

The pursuit of learning is to increase day after day.

The task is to improve one's ability and increase one's learning.

The pursuit of Tao is to decrease day after day.

The task is to return to vacuity and nonbeing.

It is to decrease and further decrease until one
reaches the point of taking no action.

No action is undertaken, and yet nothing is left
undone.

If there is action, there will certainly be
some loss. Therefore in nonaction, nothing
remains undone.

An empire is often brought to order by having no
activity.

In action, one always follows (Tao).[1]

If one (likes to) undertake activity,

That means that one does something oneself.

he is not qualified to govern the empire.

That means that one loses the controlling root.

NOTE

1. This remark also appears in Wang Pi,
chapter 49.

The sage has no fixed (personal) ideas.

He regards the people's ideas as his own.

In his action, he always follows (Tao).[1]

I treat those who are good with goodness,

And also treat those who are not good with goodness.

If each follows his functions, the good will
not be lost.

Thus goodness is attained.

That means that no one is rejected.

I am honest to those who are honest,

And I am also honest to those who are not honest.

Thus honesty is attained.

The sage, in the government of his empire, has no
subjective point of view.

His mind forms a harmonious whole with that of
his people.

They all lend their eyes and ears.[2]

All exercise their ability to hear or to see.

And he treats them all as infants.

(The sage) enables all to be in harmony and
without desire, like an infant. "Heaven and
Earth have their fixed positions and the sages
are able to carry out and complete their
abilities. They consult with the people and
spiritual beings and thus all people partici-
pate."[3] Those with ability will be accepted
and those with talent will be taken in. Where

the ability is great, one will be great, and
where the talent is honorable, one will be
honored. Things have a source and events have
a master.[4] In this way one may have the crown
jewels cover his eyes without fearing cheated,
and may have yellow fine floss-silk fill his ears
without worrying about not being respected. Why
then labor one's intelligence to investigate
the feelings of the people?

If one investigates others with intelligence,
then others will respond with their intelligence
to compete with him. If one investigates others
with distrust, others will respond with distrust
to compete with him. The hearts of the people
of the world are not necessarily the same. If
they do not dare differ in their response, then
none will act according to his own nature.[5]
There is no greater harm than the use of intelligence. "If one relies on cunning, people
will quarrel with him. If one relies on
strength, people will struggle against him."[6]
If one's cunning does not surpass others and
stands on the ground of quarrels, one will become exhausted. If one's strength does not
surpass others and stands on the ground of
struggle, one will be in danger. No one has
ever been able to tell others not to use the
cunning and strength against him."[7] This being
the case, one will be fighting alone against

others but others in thousands of tens of thousands will be fighting against him. If one increases laws and multiplies punishment, blocks people's roads and attacks their private homes, then the myriad things will lose their spontaneity and people will lose their hands and feet (ability to act). Birds above will be in disorder and fishes below will be confused. Therefore "the sage, in the government of his empire, has no subjective point of view and forms a harmonious whole with the world." That means that he does not set his mind for or against anything.[8] If he does not investigate, why will the people wish to escape? If he wants nothing, why must people comply with him? If people will neither avoid nor comply, then all will act according to their own nature. If people do not evade what they can do and try to do what they cannot, and do not evade what they are competent to do and try to do what they are not competent to do, then he who speaks will speak of what he knows, and he who acts will do what he can do. "They all lend their eyes and ears, and he treats them all as infants."

NOTES

1. This remark appears in Wang Pi, chapter 48, also. It is translated slightly differently here.

2. Chan's note (p. 187, note 4): The Wang Pi text does not have these words, but the Ho-shang Kung and Fu I texts do.

3. Book of Changes, "Appended Remarks," Part II, chapter 12.

4. Paraphrasing Lao Tzu, chapter 70.

5. Compare Analects, 13:14.

6. Quoting the Huai-nan Tzu, 14:8a

7. Paraphrasing ibid.

8. Compare Analects, 4:10.

CHAPTER 50

Man comes in to life and goes out to death.

      This means to come out of the place of life

      and to enter into the place of death.

Three out of ten[1] are companions of life.

Three out of ten are companions of death.[2]

And three out of ten in their lives lead from

      activity to death.

And for what reason?

Because of man's intensive striving after life.

I have heard that one who is a good preserver of his

      life will not meet tigers or wild buffalos,

And in fighting will not try to escape from weapons

      of war.

The wild buffalo cannot butt its horns against him,

The tiger cannot fasten its claws in him,

And weapons of war cannot thrust their blades into him.

And for what reason?

Because in him there is no room for death.

      Three out of ten means three points out of

      ten points. Let us take the way of life. Only

      three out of ten can preserve life to the utmost.

      Or take the way of death. Only three out of

      ten also will cling on to death to the utmost.

      If people seek after life too intensively, they

      will arrive at the point of no life. Those who

      are good perservers of their lives do not live

      for the sake of seeking after life.[3] Therefore

there is no room for death.

Weapons are the most destructive tools.
Similarly, rhinoceros and tigers are the most
dangerous animals. If one can prevent weapons
of war thrusting their blasts into him and the
tigers and wild buffalos from fastening their
claws and horns, then one surely does not
endanger his body with desires. Where would
there be room for death?

Worms and serpents consider the abyss to be
shallow and burrow a hole, the eagle and the
sparrowhawk consider the mountain to be low and
build their nests on top of it. Arrow and string
cannot get to them, nor can the net reach them
there. Therefore it can then be said that they
dwell where there is no room for death. However,
due to the delicious bait, they finally enter
the place of death. Is that not striving too
intensively for life? Therefore, if one is not
detached from the root by seeking and does not
change his genuineness with desires, then even
though if he enters the army, he will not be
wounded, and if he walks on land, he will not be
attacked. Truly, the infant[4] should be our model
and should be honored.

146

NOTES

1. Chan's note (p. 188, note 1): Han Fei Tzu[a]
(d. 233 B.C.) understood "ten-three" not as three out
of ten but thirteen and identified the four limbs and
the nine external cavities as factors that sustain
life, lead to death, or lead through activity to death.
See Han Fei Tzu, Ssu-pu pei-yao ed., chapter 20, 6:8a.
Most commentators and Chinese writers prefer to follow
Wang Pi, understanding "three-ten" to mean "three out
of ten." Translators are about evenly divided.

2. Chan's note (p. 180, note 3): Some Chinese
commentators have been highly imaginative in interpreting these enigmatic lines. Aside from Ho-shang
Kung...and others who have followed Han Fei Tzu, there
have been [those] who identify the thirteen as the Ten
Evils and Three Karmas of Buddhism....the sum of six
for Water and seven for Fire in the rise and fall of
the Five Agents, the Seven Feelings and Six Desires,
the twelve periods in the day plus one as their
cycle....Among modern writers, Kao Heng believes the
passage refers to the first thirty years in a hundred
as that of man's growth, the next thirty (actually
forty, but few can utilize them in full, Kao says) as
a period of neither life nor death, that is, decline,
and the remaining thirty years as a period of death...

3. Compare a similar saying in Lao Tzu, chapter
75.

4. For the infant, see Lao Tzu, chapter 55.

CHAPTER 51

Tao produces them.

Virtue fosters them.

Matter gives them physical form.

The circumstances and tendencies complete them.

> Things are produced and then fostered. They are
> fostered and then given physical form. They are
> given physical form and then completed. Whence
> are they produced? From Tao. Whereby are they
> fostered? By te[a] (virtue). Whence do they get
> physical form? From matter. What brings about
> their completion? Circumstances and tendencies.
> Only by following (Tao) can things, without ex-
> ception, obtain form, and only through circum-
> stances and tendencies can things, without ex-
> ception, be completed. For in general there is
> always a cause whereby things are produced and
> achievement completed. Since they are caused by
> something, they are all caused by Tao. Therefore
> if carried to the utmost, that too is the perfect
> Tao. If we all follow that which is caused, all
> will be just right.

Therefore the ten thousand things esteem Tao and
honor virtue.

> Tao is where things come from (or follow). Te
> is what things attain. Only by following Tao
> does one attain te. Therefore it is said that
> if one does not attain Tao, one is not esteemed.[1]

148

It is harmful to lose <u>te</u>. If one does not attain
<u>te</u>, one is not honored.

Tao is esteemed and virtue is honored without anyone's
order!

They always come spontaneously.

Order...act.[2]

Therefore Tao produces them and virtue fosters them.
They rear them and develop them.
They give them security and give them peace.
They nurture them and protect them.

It means that all things are complete in substance, each enjoying the protection of Tao and
its substance will not be harmed.

Tao produces them but does not take possession of
them.

It acts but does not rely on its own ability.

One acts but does not take possession of them.

It leads them but does not master them.

This is called profound and secret virtue.

One achieves <u>te</u> but does not know its ruler.
It comes from the hidden and dark realm and
therefore we call it the profound and secret
virtue.

NOTES

1. The words <u>shih</u>[b] (to lose) and <u>tsun</u>[c] (to esteem) are reversed in the translation, following T'ao Hung-ch'ing.

2. The commentary here is too corrupt to make any sense. I Shun-ting and other commentators believe that it is a later interpolation. See Hatano, III, p. 23.

CHAPTER 52

There was a beginning of the universe

Which may be called the Mother of the universe.[1]

He who has found the Mother (Tao)

And thereby understands her sons (things),

And having understood the sons,

Still keeps to its mother,

Will be free from danger throughout his lifetime.

> Mother is the roots and son is the branches.
> One should find the roots in order to understand
> the branches, but one should not cast away the
> roots in order to pursue the branches.

Close the mouth.

Shut the doors (of cunning and desires).

> Out of the mouth come things and desires.
> Through the door come things and desires.

And to the end of life there will be (peace) without
toil.

> As one is without ado and is always at leisure,
> "Therefore to the end of life there will be
> (peace) without toil."

Open the mouth.

Meddle with affairs.

And to the end of life there will be no salvation.

> If one does not close the source but meddles
> with affairs, then "to the end of life there
> will be no salvation."

Seeing what is small is called enlightenment.

Keeping to weakness is called strength.

The task[2] of governing does not lie in the great.

Seeing the great does not mean that one is enlightened; only by seeing the small can one be enlightened. Keeping to strength does not make one strong; only by keeping to weakness can one be strong.

Use the light.

Manifest the Tao in order to remove the delusions of the people.

Revert to enlightenment.

This means not to probe into things with the light.

And thereby avoid danger to one's life--

This is called practicing the eternal.

This means the eternity of Tao.

NOTES

1. Some editions have this commentary: When the beginning is good, nourishment and nurture will be good. Therefore when there is a beginning of the universe, it can be the mother of the universe.

2. Kung[a] here does not mean accomplishment but work, according to Hatano, III, p. 30.

CHAPTER 53

If I had but little[1] knowledge

I should, in walking on a broad way,

Fear getting off the road.

> It means that if I had but little knowledge and
> walked on a broad way in the world, the only
> thing to be feared is behavior.[2]

Broad ways are extremely even,

But people are fond of bypaths.

> This means that the great Tao is even and broad,
> but people still avoid it and do not follow it
> but love to follow bad by-paths. How much more
> if people behave in such a way as to block the
> broad way? Therefore it is said, "Broad ways
> are extremely even, but people are fond of
> bypaths."

The courts are exceedingly splendid,

> Courts mean palaces, and "splendid" means clean
> and beautiful.

While the fields are exceedingly weedy,

And the granaries are exceedingly empty.

> When the palaces are clean and beautiful, then
> the fields are exceedingly weedy and the
> granaries are exceedingly empty. One establishes
> the one (the ruler) but harms the life of the
> people.

Elegant clothes are worn,

Sharp weapons are carried,

Foods and drinks are enjoyed beyond limit,

And wealth and treasures are accumulated in excess.

This is robbery and extravagance.

This is indeed not Tao (the Way).

When things are obtained in violation of Tao,

they are all evil. Being evil means robbery.

When extravagance is obtained in violation

of Tao, that is usurpation. Therefore, to

use violation of Tao to explain violation of

Tao is nothing but robbery and extravagance.

NOTES

1. Chan's note (p. 194, note 1): The term chieh-jan[a] can mean "firmly," "wisely," "especially," "hastily," and so on, and support for each can be found in ancient literature. But in spite of Ho-shang Kung's understanding of it as "great," most commentators, from Ch'eng Hsüan-ying down, have preferred to follow Chang Chan's commentaries on the Lieh Tzu, 4:2a, where it is understood as "small" or "subtle."

2. Shih[b] (getting off the road) is interpreted by Wang Pi as "to behave," "to act," that is, to interfere with things. For a similar interpretation of shih and wei[c] (to act), see Wang Pi, chapters 29 and 64.

CHAPTER 54

He who is well established (in Tao) cannot be pulled
away.

He cannot be pulled away because he first makes
the root firm and strong and then devotes his
attention to the branches.

He who has a firm grasp (of Tao) cannot be separated
from it.

He cannot be separated because he does not
desire a great deal but acts according to his
ability.

Thus from generation to generation his ancestral
sacrifice will never be suspended.

If from generation to generation sons and grand-
sons transmit this Tao for sacrifice, then those
ancestral sacrifices will never be suspended.

When one cultivates virtue in his person, it becomes
genuine virtue.

When one cultivates virtue in his family, it becomes
overflowing virtue.

This means that one starts by cultivating oneself
to reach others. If one cultivates virtue in
his person, then one becomes genuine. If one
cultivates virtue in his family, it becomes
overflowing virtue. If one can cultivate Tao
without abandoning it, then what one does for
others will become great.

When one cultivates virtue in his community, it

becomes lasting virtue.

When one cultivates virtue in his country, it becomes
abundant virtue.

When one cultivates virtue in the world, it becomes
universal.

Therefore the person should be viewed as a person.

The family should be viewed as a family.

The community should be viewed as a community.

The country should be viewed as a country.

They are all like that.

And the world should be viewed as the world.

This means to use the mind of the people to view
the Tao of the world. In the Tao of the world,
whether things are for or against one, whether
lucky or unlucky, they all are also like the
Tao of man.

How do I know this to be the case in the world?
Through this.[1]

"This" refers to what is said earlier. It means
that one looks at oneself in order to understand
the world and does not look to the outside.

That is what is meant in saying, "One may know
the world without going out of doors."[2]

156

NOTES

1. Chan's note (p. 196, note 2): Most commentators agree that "this" refers to the cultivation of virtue in the person, in the family, and so forth.

2. Quoting <u>Lao Tzu</u>, chapter 47.

CHAPTER 55

He who possesses virtue in abundance

May be compared to an infant.

Poisonous insects[1] will not sting him.

Fierce beasts will not seize him.

Birds of prey will not strike him.

> An infant seeks nothing and desires none. He
> does not offend the myriad things. Therefore
> he is a being who will not be stung by poisonous
> insects. He who possesses virtue in abundance
> does not offend things. Therefore there is
> nothing to harm his wholeness.

His bones are weak, his sinews tender, but his grasp
is firm.

> Because of weakness, he can grasp firmly.

He does not yet know the union of male and female,

But his organ[2] is aroused,

> To arouse means to grow. There is nothing to
> harm his body and therefore he can grow to
> completion.[3] It means that if one possesses
> virtue in abundance, nothing can harm his te
> or change his genuineness. Those who are weak
> and do not contend and will therefore not be
> broken are all like this.

This means that his essence is at its height.

He may cry all day without becoming hoarse.

> He does not wish to contend or desire. There-
> fore he may cry all day without becoming hoarse.

This means that his (natural) harmony is perfect.

To know harmony means to be in accord with the eternal.

> The constancy of things consists in harmony.

> Therefore if one knows harmony, one will attain
> constancy.

To be in accord with the eternal means to be

> enlightened.

> Neither light nor dark, neither warm nor cool--
> that is constancy.

> Without form and invisible--that means
> enlightenment.

To force the growth of life means ill omen.[4]

> The growth of life cannot be forced. If it is,
> evil will result.

For the mind to employ the vital force without

> restraint means violence.

> The heart should remain empty. One who employs
> vital force will be violent.

After things reach their prime, they begin to grow

> old,

Which means being contrary to Tao.

Whatever is contrary to Tao will soon perish.

NOTES

1. Chan's note (p. 198, note 1): Following the Ho-shang Kung text. [Some] texts have "poisonous insects." Chiang Hsi-ch'ang mentions fifty texts that have "poisonous insects." In place of this expression, the Wang Pi text has "wasps, scorpions, and snakes." These words appear in the Ho-shang Kung's commentary. Probably they got into the Wang Pi text by mistake.

2. Chan's note (p. 198, note 2): Also following the Ho-shang Kung text and forty-five other texts (according to Chiang). Wang Pi's text has ch'ùan[a] (complete), which sounds like the word for the male organ but makes no sense here.

3. Wang Pi's interpretation: "Grow to completion" instead of "Organ is aroused."

4. Chan's note (p. 198, note 3): Hsiang[b] (good omen) was occasionally used in ancient literature in the opposite sense. For example, see Tso chuan, Duke Chao[c], 18th year.

CHAPTER 56

He who knows does not speak.

    This is so because one follows <u>Tzu-jan</u>.

He who speaks does not know.

    Because he would create trouble.

Close the mouth.

Shut the doors.

Blunt the sharpness.

    This means one keeps and protects one's own
    nature.

Untie the tangles.

    This means one keeps oneself free from causes
    for quarrel.

Soften the light.

    If one is not especially prominent in any way,
    others will not particularly quarrel with him
    at all.

Become one with the dusty world.

    If one does not particularly despise anything,
    then others will not particularly humiliate him
    at all.

This is called profound identification.

Therefore it is impossible either to be intimate and
    close to him or to be distant and indifferent
    to him.

    If it is possible to be intimate and close, then
    it is possible to be distant and indifferent.

It is impossible either to benefit him or to harm him.

If one can be benefited, one can also be harmed.

It is impossible either to honor him or to disgrace him.

If one can be honored, one can also be disgraced.

For this reason he is honored by the world.

Nothing can be added to him.

CHAPTER 57

Govern the state with correctness.

Operate the army with surprise tactics.

Administer the empire by engaging in no activity.

If one governs the state with Tao, the state will be at peace. If one governs the state with correctness, there will be craftiness and justice. With nonactivity one can administer the world. In a previous chapter it is said, "An empire is often brought to order by having no activity. If one (likes to) undertake activity, he is not qualified to govern the empire."[1] Therefore, if one governs the world with correctness, one cannot administer the world and operate the army with surprise tactics. If one governs the country with Tao, one honors the roots so as to put an end to the branches. If one governs the world with correctness, one imposes punishment in order to devote oneself to the branches. The root will not be established and the branches will be shallow, and there will be nothing for the people. Therefore one is forced to resort to operate the army with the surprise tactics.

How do I know that this should be so?

Through this:

The more taboos and prohibitions there are in the world,

The poorer the people will be.

The more sharp weapons the people have,

The more troubled the state will be.

> Sharp weapons are generally those which benefit oneself.[2] When the people are strong, the state is weak.

The more cunning and skill man possesses,

The more vicious things will appear.

> If people are highly intelligent (cunning), cunning and falsehood will arise. If cunning and falsehood arise, then evil will occur.

The more laws and orders are made prominent,

The more thieves and robbers there will be.

> If by correctness one wishes to put an end to evil, then one must use surprise tactics to operate the army, and there will be many regulations and taboos. The desire is to reduce poverty to shame, but people will be all the poorer. Sharp weapons are intended to strengthen the country, but the state will be more and more confused. All this is because the roots are abandoned in order to manage the branches. Hence these results.

Therefore the sage says:

I take no action and the people of themselves are transformed.

I love tranquility and the people of themselves become correct.

I engage in no activity and the people of themselves

become prosperous.

I have no desires and the people of themselves
become simple.

What the ruler desires will be immediately
followed by the people. If my desire is to be
without desire, then the people will also be
without desire and will of themselves become
simple. These four are (examples) of honoring
the roots so as to put an end to the branches.

NOTES

1. Quoting Lao Tzu, chapter 48.

2. Yen Ling-feng suggests that chi[a] (self) here
should read min[b] (people). This seems reasonable
because it follows Lao Tzu closely. A similar
suggestion is made in Hatano, III, p. 48.

CHAPTER 58

When the government is nondiscriminative and dull,

The people are contented and generous.

>This means that he who rules well is without

>form, without name, and without measures that

>can be mentioned. He is nondiscriminative

>and dull, and he ultimately achieves great order.

>Therefore it is said that "His government is

>nondiscriminative and dull." His people will

>not compete or strive for anything, and they

>will be broad and liberal, and contented and

>generous. Therefore it is said that the people

>are contented and generous."

When the government is searching and discriminative,

The people are disappointed and contentious.

>[When the government] establishes legal measures

>and makes prominent rewards and punishments

>to examine treachery and falsehood, it is said

>to be searching and discriminative. The ruler

>being discriminative and divisive, the people

>will become competitive. Therefore it is said,

>"The people are disappointed and contentious."

Calamity is that upon which happiness depends;

Happiness is that in which calamity is latent.

Who knows when the limit will be reached?

Is there no correctness (used to govern the world)?

>Who knows the limit of good government? Only

>when there is no correctness to be imposed and

when there are neither forms nor names will the world be greatly transformed without discrimination. This is the limit.

Then the correct again becomes the perverse.

If one "governs the state with correctness," one will naturally "operate the army with surprise tactics."[1] Therefore it is said, "The correct again becomes the perverse."

And the good will again become evil.

If one establishes goodness to bring harmony in the myriad things, there will naturally be the danger of evil.

The people have been deluded for a long time.

This is to say that as the people have been deluded and have lost the Tao for a long time, it is not good to demand from them correctness and goodness right away.

Therefore the sage is as pointed as a square but does not pierce.

To lead the people with the pointed square and to remove their evil, but not to use the pointed square to pierce things--this is what is meant by saying, "The great square has no corners."[2]

He is as acute as a knife but does not cut.

To be acute means to be incorruptible,[3] and to cut means to harm. It means to purify the people with incorruptibility and to enable them to remove their evil and uncleanliness but not to hurt them with incorruptibility.

He is as straight as an unbent line but does not ex-

tend.

This is to lead the people with uprightness and

to enable them to remove their depravity but not

to stir up things by inflexibility. This is what

is meant by the saying, "What is most straight

seems to be crooked."[4]

He is as bright as light but does not dazzle.

This is to use light to reveal wherein the

people are deluded but not to use light to

search for their secrets. This is what is

meant by saying, "The Tao which is bright

appears to be dark."[5] All these are to honor

the root so as to put an end to the branches.

One does not need to apply oneself to anything

and all will return to·its own.

NOTES

1. Quoting _Lao Tzu_, chapter 57.

2. Quoting _Lao Tzu_, chapter 41.

3. _Lien_[a] (acute) is here interpreted by Wang Pi
in the sense of being incorruptible.

4. Quoting _Lao Tzu_, chapter 45.

5. Quoting _Lao Tzu_, chapter 41.

CHAPTER 59

To rule people and to serve Heaven is nothing better
than to be frugal.

"Nothing better" means that nothing will surpass
it. Frugality refers to the farmer. He manages
his fieldwork and eliminates the weeds so that
the crops become standardized and uniform. He
preserves the natural state of things. He does
not worry about the trouble of the fallowland,
but removes the cause of the trouble of the
fallowland. (The sage) receives the mandate of
Heaven; below, he soothes the hundred families.
There is nothing better than the example mentioned above.

Only by being frugal can one recover quickly.

This means to recover constancy early.

To recover quickly means to accumulate virtue heavily.

Only by heavily accumulating virtue and by not
wanting to hurry can one recover his constancy
early. Therefore it is said, "To recover quickly
means to accumulate virtue heavily."

By the heavy accumulation of virtue one can overcome
everything.

If one can overcome everything, then he will acquire
a capacity the limit of which is beyond anyone's
knowledge.

Because Tao is limitless.

When his capacity is beyond anyone's knowledge, he

is fit to rule a state.

It is impossible to keep the state by ruling
it with limits.

He who possesses the Mother (Tao) of the state will
last long.

That which gives a state peace is known as the
Mother. To accumulate virtue heavily is only
to plan for the root and then devote oneself to
the branches.[1] Then one can come to the (right)
end.

This means that the roots are deep and the stalks are
firm, which is the way of long life and
everlasting vision.[2]

NOTES

1. A similar statement is found in Wang Pi, chapters 38, 39, 52, and 57.

2. Chan's note (p. 205, note 2): "Long life and lasting vision" simply means long life....Waley contends that "fixed staring" (his translation) was used by the Taoists as a method of inducing trances. This interpretation is accurate in regard to later religious Taoists, but errs in reading yoga into the Lao Tzu. Waley interprets frugality as "laying up a store," and goes on to say that this 'laying of the new upon the old' is here used as a symbol for the reinforcing of one's stock of vital energy by quietist practice" (p. 213). He is here following Ho-shang Kung's commentary. This interpretation puts much yoga indeed into the Lao Tzu; many would join Duyvendak in rejecting Waley's interpretation.

CHAPTER 60

Ruling a big country is like cooking a small fish.

That means not to disturb. If one is hasty, one

harms much, but if one remains quiet, one pre-

serves one's genuineness.[1] Therefore the larger

the land is, the quieter the rulers has to be.

Only then can one reach the heart of the

multitude fully.

If Tao is employed to rule the empire,

Spiritual being will lose their supernatural power.

To rule a great empire, one should behave like

cooking a small fish. If one rules over the

empire in accordance with Tao, then the spiritual

beings will lose their supernatural power.

Not that they lose their spiritual power,

But their spiritual power can no longer harm people.

This means that the spiritual power does not harm

Tzu-jan. If things abide by Tzu-jan, the spir-

itual power cannot do anything to them. As the

spiritual power cannot do anything to them, one

does not know that spiritual power is spiritual

power.

Not only will their supernatural power not harm people,

But the sage also will not harm people.

When one is in harmony with Tao, then the spir-

itual power will not harm people. If spiritual

power does not harm people, one does not know that

spiritual power is spiritual power. If one is

in harmony with Tao, then the sage will also not harm the people. If the sage does not harm the people, then one does not know that the sage is a sage. That means the people do not know about the spiritual power of spiritual beings or the sagacity of the sage. When the ruler relies on the net of power to deal with things, the government is on the decline. To bring about the situation of not knowing the spiritual power of spiritual beings or the sagacity of the sage is the ultimate of Tao.

When both do not harm each other,

Virtue will be accumulated in both for the benefit (of the people).

If spiritual power does not harm people, then the sage will also not harm people. If the sage will not harm the people, then spiritual power will also not harm the people. Therefore it is said, "When both do not harm each other, spiritual beings and the sage will be in accord with Tao "for the benefit (of the people)."

NOTE

1. A similar statement is found in Wang Pi, chapter 45.

CHAPTER 61

A big country may be compared to the lower part of a
river.

If a sea occupies the position of bigness but
stays low, a hundred rivers will flow into it.

If a big country occupies a position of bigness
but stays low, the world will flow into it.

Therefore it is said, "A big country may be compared to the lower part of a river."

It is the converging point of the world.

It means the place to which the world converges.

It is the female of the world.

If one is quiet and does not seek anything,
things will naturally return to him.

The female always overcomes the male by tranquility,
And by tranquility she is underneath.

Because of her tranquility, (the female) can
remain low. Female means the feminine sex. The
male is hasty, restless, and greedy. The female
is always tranquil and can therefore overcome
the male. Because of her quietness and, furthermore, her ability to stay low, things move
toward her.

A big state can take over a small state if it places
itself below the small state;

"A big state places itself below" means that the
big state places itself below the small state.

The small state will submit to the big state.

And the small state can take over a big state if it

    places itself below the big state.

    That means that the big state will take in the

    small state.

Thus some, by placing themselves below, take over

    (others),

And some, by being (naturally) low, take over (other

    states).

    That means that if only each state will cultivate

    the humble and the lowly, each will find peace

    and ease in one's own place.

After all, what a big state wants is but to annex

    and herd others,

And what a small state wants is merely to join and

    serve others.

Since both big and small states get what they want,

The big state should place itself low.

    If a small state cultivates the lowly, it can

    preserve itself and that is all, but it cannot

    thereby cause the world to return to it. But

    when a big state cultivates the lowly, then the

    world returns to it. Therefore it is said,

    "Since both big and small states get what they

    want, the big state should place itself low."

CHAPTER 62

Tao is the storehouse[1] of all things.

> Ao[a] means the sun covered by cloud.[2] That means
> one can get protection

It is the good man's treasure

> Treasure is to be used.

  and the bad man's refuge

> Refuge means to be preserved.

Fine words can buy honor,[3]

And fine deeds can gain respect from others.

> That means Tao is ahead of all things. There is
> nothing more precious than Tao. Although there
> are treasures and jade horses, nothing is equal
> to Tao. When it is praised with fine words it
> can take away the sale of all goods. Therefore
> it is said, "Fine words can buy (honor)." When
> it is honored and I practice Tao, people will
> respond to it even at a distance of a thousand
> li.[4] Therefore it is said, "[Fine deeds] can
> gain respect from others."

Even if a man is bad, when has (Tao) rejected him?

> Bad men should be protected. Tao will give them
> freedom.

Therefore on the occasion of crowning an emperor or
installing the three ministers,[5]

> That means to honor and practice Tao.

Rather than present large pieces of jade preceded
by teams of four horses,

It is better to kneel and offer this Tao.

> This is the Tao mentioned earlier. It means
> that on the occasion of crowning an emperor or
> installing the three ministers, to honor those
> positions and to respect the men is the way to
> practice Tao. Nothing is more honorable than
> this. Therefore, "Rather than present large
> pieces of jade preceded by teams of four horses,
> it is better to kneel and offer this Tao."

Why did the ancients highly value this Tao?

Did they not say, "Those who seek shall have it and
those who sin shall be freed"?

For this reason it is valued by the world.

> If one seeks, one will find. If one seeks
> freedom, one will find freedom. This applies
> everywhere. Therefore it is valued by the world.

NOTES

1. Chan's note (p. 210, note 1): Literally, the southwestern corner of the house, the most highly honored place in the house, where family worship was carried out, grains and treasures were stored, and so forth.

2. Wang Pi does not interpret <u>ao</u> as the storehouse.

3. Chan's note (p. 210, note 2): The texts have <u>shih-tsun-hsing</u>[b] (buy honorable acts) and punctuate after <u>tsun</u>, making the sentence read: "Fine acts can sell, and honorable acts...." Yü Yüeh, on the authority of the <u>Huai-nan Tzu</u>, 12:11b and 18:9a, has added the second word "fine." The present translation follows him....

4. A <u>li</u>[c] is one-third of a mile.

5. Chan's note (p. 211, note 4): Grand tutor, grand preceptor, and grand protector.

CHAPTER 63

Act without action.

Do without ado.

Taste without tasting.

This is to take nonaction as the dwelling place,
to teach without words,[1] and to take tasteless-
ness for taste. This is the ultimate principle
of government.

Whether it is big or small, many or few, repay hatred
with virtue.

Slight hatred is not worth repaying. Great
hatred, however, is condemned by the whole world.
To be in accord with what is shared by the whole
world [in denouncing hatred] is virtue.

Prepare for the difficult while it is still easy.

Deal with the big while it is still small.

Difficult undertakings have always started with what
is easy.

And great undertakings have always started with
what is small.

Therefore the sage never strives for the great,

And thereby the great is achieved.

He who makes rash promises surely lacks faith.

He who takes things too easily will surely encounter
much difficulty.

For this reason even the sage regards things as
difficult.

Even with the capacity of the sage, it is still

difficult to prepare (for the difficult) while

it is easy and (for the big) while it is small.

How much more for those without the ability of

the sage to wish to neglect this? Therefore

it is said, "Even (the sage) regards this as

difficult."

And therefore he encounters no difficulty.

NOTE

1. The same comment appears in Wang Pi,

chapters 17, 23. In chapter 23 chü^a (dwelling place)

appears as chün^b (master). Compare Lao Tzu, chapters

2 and 43.

CHAPTER 64

What remains still is easy to hold.

What is not yet manifest is easy to plan for.

"Because of this stillness, one should never
forget the danger. In holding on to a thing,
never forget its demise."[1] This is to plan
without effort. Therefore it is said to be easy.

What is brittle is easy to crack.

What is minute is easy to scatter.

Although one loses nonbeing and enters into being,
since it is minute and brittle, it is not enough
to make a great effort. Therefore it is easy.
These four explain how one should be careful
about the end. One should not fail to hold on
because it is nothing, and one should not fail
to scatter because it is subtle. Not to hold
on to nonbeing will produce being, and not to
scatter subtleness will produce bigness. Therefore if one carefully considers the danger at
the end as one considers the trouble in the
beginning, one will never fail.

Deal with things before they appear.

That means that there is not yet any omen of
its stillness.

Put things in order before disorder arises.

That refers to the subtle and the brittle.

A tree as big as a man's embrace grows from a tiny
shoot.

A tower of nine stories begins with a heap of earth.

The journey of a thousand li[a] starts from where
one stands.

He who takes action fails.

He who grasps things loses them.

One should remove the subtle with careful consideration of the end and remove disorder with
careful consideration of the subtle. If one
tries to put things in order by action, and
holds on to things by means of forms and names,
difficulties will arise. Then cleverness and
depravity will multiply. Thus one will fail.

For this reason the sage takes no action and therefore does not fail.

He grasps nothing and therefore he does not lose
anything.

People in their handling of affairs often fail when
they are about to succeed.

Because one is not careful about the end.

If one remains as careful at the end as he was at
the beginning, there will be no failure.

Therefore the sage desires to have no desire.

He does not value rare treasures.

Though greed and desire may be small, strife
and aspiration will arise because of them.

Though rare treasures may be small, greed
and theft arise because of them.

He learns to be unlearned,[2] and returns to what the
multitude has missed (Tao).

To be capable without learning is <u>Tzu-jan</u>. This explains that those who do not learn (to be unlearned) will miss.[3] Therefore, "He learns to be unlearned, and returns to what the multitude has missed."

Thus he supports all things in their natural state but does not take any action.

NOTES

1. Quoting the <u>Book of Changes</u>, "Appended Remarks," Part II, chapter 5.

2. Chan's note (p. 215, note 6): Wang Pi understands the expression "learn not learn" to mean that the sage learns without learning. Ho-shang Kung interprets it to mean that the sage learns what the multitude cannot learn.

3. This sentence is very obscure.

CHAPTER 65

In ancient times those who practiced Tao well

Did not seek to enlighten the people, but to make

them ignorant.

Enlightenment means having many points of view

and being clever and cunning so as to obscure

one's simplicity. Ignorance means having no

knowledge (cunning), keeping to the true state

of things, and following Tzu-jan.

People are difficult to govern because they have too

much knowledge.

If people have too much knowledge (cunning) and

are clever and deceitful, it will be difficult

to govern them.

Therefore he who rules the state through knowledge

is a robber of the state.

Knowledge is the same as government. One who

governs with knowledge is called a robber.

Therefore it is called knowledge. People are

difficult to govern because they have too much

knowledge. One should strive to close the mouth

and shut the doors,[1] and "cause people to be

without knowledge or desire."[2] If one tries to

arouse people by cunning and devices, one's evil

mind is already aroused, and if one further uses

clever tricks to prevent the falsehood of people,

people will be aware of his tricks and will

immediately try to get away from them. Thus

thoughts will be secret and clever and their
treachery and falsehood will multiply. Therefore it is said, "He who rules the state
through knowledge is a robber of the state."
He who rules a state not through knowledge is a
blessing to the state.
One who knows these two things also (knows) the
standard.
Always to know the standard is called profound and
secret virtue.
Virtue becomes deep and far-reaching. Standard
means agreement. What is agreed upon now and
in former times cannot be abolished. "If
one knows the standard, it is called profound
and secret virtue. Virtue becomes deep and
far-reaching."
And with it all things return to their original
state.
That means to return to their true state.
Then complete harmony will be reached.

NOTES

1. Quoting <u>Lao Tzu</u>, chapters 52 and 56.

2. Quoting <u>Lao Tzu</u>, chapter 3.

CHAPTER 66

The great rivers and seas are kings of all mountain
streams

Because they skillfully stay below them.

That is why they can be their kings.

Therefore, to be the superior of the people,

One must, in the use of words, place himself below
them.

And to be ahead of the people,

One must, in one's own person, follow them.

Therefore the sage places himself above the people,
and they do not feel his weight.

He places himself in front of them, and the people
do not harm him.

Therefore the world rejoices in praising him without
getting tired of it.

It is precisely because he does not compete that
the world cannot compete with him.

[As in chapter 31, there is no commentary by
Wang Pi in this chapter.]

CHAPTER 67

All the world says that my Tao is great and does not
   seem to resemble (the ordinary).[1]

It is precisely because it is great that it does not
   resemble (the ordinary).

If it did resemble, it would have been small for a
   long time.

   Being small for a long time means that smallness
   has already lasted for a long time. To resemble
   will lose that which makes a thing great.

   Therefore it is said, "If it did resemble, it
   would have been small for a long time."

I have three treasures. Guard and keep them:

The first is deep love,[2]

The second is frugality,

And the third is not to dare to be ahead of the world.

Because of deep love, one is courageous.

   "Deep love helps one to win in the case of
   attack and to be firm in the case of defense."[3]

   Therefore one is courageous.

Because of frugality, one is generous.

   If one loves thrift and keeps down expenses,
   then the world will not be exhausted. Therefore
   one is generous.

Because of not daring to be ahead of the world, one
   becomes the leader of the world.

   Only if one places oneself in the background and
   puts oneself away will all people come to one.[4]

Then one can "establish oneself for the benefit
of the world"[5] and thus be the leader.

Now, to be courageous by forsaking deep love,
This means that one is preferred to the other.

To be generous by forsaking frugality,

And to be ahead of the world by forsaking following
behind--

This is fatal.

For deep love helps one to win in the case of attack,
Being charitable and not avoiding difficulties,
one therefore conquers.

And to be firm in the case of defense.

When Heaven is to save a person,

Heaven will protect him through deep love.

NOTES

1. Chan's note (p. 220, note 2): The term pu-hsiao[a] (not to resemble) is open to many possible interpretations: "unworthy," "seems to be like folly," "indescribable," "cannot be distinguished," and so on.

2. Chan's note (p. 220, note 3): The word tz'u[b] (deep love) has been variously translated as "pity," "love," "compassion," and so on. It simply means great or deep love. In chapters 18 and 19 it is used with special reference to the love of parents for children. Here it is used with reference to all men.

3. Read ch'en[c] (to spread out) as chan[d] (to attack), to conform with the Lao Tzu text below.

4. Referring to Lao Tzu, chapter 7.

5. Quoting the Book of Changes, "Appended Remarks," Part I, chapter 11.

CHAPTER 68

A skillful leader of troops is not oppressive with
   his military strength.
   A leader of troops is the general of soldiers.
   What a man of military strength likes best is
   to be ahead of people and to attack people.
A skillful fighter does not become angry.
   Following behind but not getting in the front,[1]
   responding but not singing first, one will not
   be angry.
A skillful conqueror does not compete with people.
   That means not competing.
One who is skillful in using men puts himself below
   them.
This is called the virtue of noncompeting.
This is called the strength to use men.
   If people use others but do not put themselves
   below them, strength cannot be used.
This is called matching Heaven, the highest principle
   of old.

NOTE

1. Referring to Lao Tzu, chapter 7.

CHAPTER 69

The strategists say:

"I dare not take the offensive but I take the

    defensive;

I dare not advance an inch but I retreat a foot."

This means:

To march without formation,

    That means not to stop advancing.[1]

To stretch one's arm without showing it,

To confront enemies without seeming to meet them,

    To march means to walk in battle formation. It

    means to practice modesty, sympathy, and deep

    love, and not to dare to go ahead of things.

    To fight a battle is similar to marching

    without formation, to stretch one's arm without

    seeming to meet them, to hold weapons without

    seeming to have them, and to confront enemies

    without seeming to meet them. All this means

    that there is no one who could oppose him.

To hold weapons without seeming to have them.

There is no greater disaster than to make light of

    the enemy.

Making light of the enemy will destroy my treasures.

    This means that my sympathy, deep love, and

    modesty are not intended to achieve strength

    so there will be no enemy in the world. If I

    cannot help and finally arrive at the point of

    making light of the enemy, that will be a great

disaster for me. Treasures mean the three treasures.[2] Therefore it is said, "It will destroy my treasures."

Therefore when armies are mobilized and issues joined, The man who is sorry over the fact will win.

To mobilize means to rise in action and to join issues means to face each other. The man who is sorry will have sympathy for others and will not seek benefit or avoid harm. He will therefore win.

NOTES

1. An obscure sentence, Hatano (III, p. 94) thinks that this note probably belongs to Ho-shang Kung's commentary on the Lao Tzu and has been inadvertently inserted here.

2. Wang Pi may be thinking of the three treasures in Lao Tzu, chapter 67.

CHAPTER 70

My doctrines are very easy to understand and very
easy to practice,

But none in the world can understand or practice
them.

It is possible to know (the world) without
going out of the door or looking out the win-
dow.[1] That is why it says it is very easy to
understand. One accomplishes without any
action.[2] Therefore it is said, "My doctrine
is very easy to practice." It is said that
"none in the world can understand them" because people are deluded by hotheadedness and
desire, and it is said that "none in the world
can practice them" because people are deluded
by glory and gain.

My doctrines have a source (Nature); my deeds have
a master (Tao).

By source is meant the source of the myriad
things. By ruler is meant the lord of the
myriad things.

It is because people do not understand this that
they do not understand me.

Since these words have a source and deeds have
a master, he who has the knowledge cannot help
knowing them.

Few people know me, and therefore I am highly

valued.

Since my words have come from such depth,
those who can understand them are rare. The
fewer there are who know me, the less will
there be any match for me. Therefore it is
said, "Few people know me, and therefore I
am highly valued."

Therefore the sage wears a coarse cloth on top and
carries jade within his bosom.

Those who wear coarse clothing "become one
with the dusty world,"[3] and those who carry
jade treasure its genuineness. The reason
the sage is difficult to understand is because
he is one with the dusty world and is not
different, and he carries jade within his
bosom and does not change. Therefore he is
hard to know and is highly valued.

NOTES

1. Paraphrasing Lao Tzu, chapter 47.
2. Ibid.
3. Quoting Lao Tzu, chapters 4, 56.

CHAPTER 71

To know that you do not know is the best.

To pretend to know when you do not know is a

    disease.

    Not to know that knowledge is not reliable

    would be a disease.

Only when one recognizes this disease as a disease

    can one be free from the disease.

The sage is free from the disease.

Because he recognizes this disease to be disease,

    he is free from it.[1]

NOTE

1. In the <u>Tao-te chen-ching chi-chu</u>, there
is this comment by Wang Pi on this sentence: Those
who recognize this disease to be disease are
therefore free from the disease.

CHAPTER 72

When the people do not fear what is dreadful,

Then what is greatly dreadful will descend on them.

Do not reduce the living space of their dwellings.

Do not oppress their lives.

> Dwelling means to be tranquil and taking no
> action, and to live means to be modest and
> not full. If one deviates from purity and
> tranquility, practices fierceness and desires,
> discards one's modesty, and gives rein to power
> and violence, then things will become disturbed
> and people will avoid him. People can no
> longer be controlled by power. As people
> cannot stand this power, both above and below
> will totally collapse. Heaven will execute
> him. Therefore it is said, "When the people
> do not fear what is dreadful, then what is
> greatly dreadful will descend on them. Do not
> reduce the living space of their dwelling.
> Do not oppress their lives." It means that
> power cannot be relied on.

It is because you do not oppress them

> This means not to oppress oneself.

that they are not oppressed.

> As one does not oppress oneself, the whole
> world will not oppress him.

Therefore the sage knows himself but does not show
himself.

He does not himself show what he knows so that
he may shine and be powerful.

He loves himself but does not exalt himself.

If one sets too high a value on oneself, then
his dwelling will be reduced and his life
oppressed.

Therefore he rejects the one but accepts the other.

CHAPTER 73

He who is brave in daring will be killed.

One will surely not have a natural death.

He who is brave in not daring will live.

One will surely reach the full length[1] of one's life.

Of these two, one is advantageous and one is harmful.

Both cases show bravery but the applications of bravery are different. The advantage and harm are different. Therefore it is said, "One is advantageous and one is harmful."

Who knows why Heaven dislikes what it dislikes?

Even the sage considers it a difficult question.

Shui[a] means "which person?" It means: Who can know the reason why the world dislikes things.[2] Only the sage knows. The knowledge of the sage still makes it difficult to be brave in daring. How much more for one who has not the knowledge of the sage but who wants to act with bravery and daring? Therefore it is said, "The sage considers it a difficult question."

The Way of Heaven does not compete, and yet it skillfully achieves victory.

"It is precisely because he does not compete that the world connot compete with him."[3]

198

and yet skillfully responds to things.

To follow will result in good fortune and to oppose will result in evil fortune. One does not speak and yet skillfully responds to things.

It comes to you without your invitation.

If one places oneself in a lower position, things will come of themselves.

It is not anxious about things and yet it plans well.

Heaven hangs out images so that fortune and misfortune can be seen. Before things occur, one has to plan for them. When there is stillness, one does not forget the danger,[4] and when a thing is not yet manifest, one plans for it.[5] Therefore it is said, "It is not anxious about things and yet it plans well."

Heaven's net is indeed vast.

Though its meshes are wide, it misses nothing.

NOTES

1. Ch'i[b] (equal) here reads chi[c], to complete, to fulfill, or to accomplish, as in Wang Pi, chapter 17.

2. In Lieh Tzu, 6:4a, Lao Tzu's saying, "Who knows why Heaven dislike what it dislikes" is quoted. In his commentary on this quotation, Chang Chan quoted Wang Pi as saying, "It means: Who can know the will of Heaven? Only the sage knows."

3. Quoting Lao Tzu, chapter 22.

4. Book of Changes, "Appended Remarks," Part II, chapter 5.

5. Compare similar comments in Lao Tzu, chapter 64, and Wang Pi's commentary on its opening sentences.

CHAPTER 74

The people are not afraid of death.

Why, then, threaten them with death?

Suppose the people are always afraid of death and
    we can seize those who are vicious and kill
    them.

Who would dare to do so?

    To create disorder and uncommon tactics is
    called vicious.

There is always the master executioner (Heaven)
    who kills.

To undertake executions for the master executioner
    is like hewing wood for the master carpenter.

Whoever undertakes to hew wood for the master
    carpenter rarely escapes injuring his own
    hands.

    He who opposes is resented and hated by those
    who follow. Unkindness is disliked by all.
    Therefore it is said, "There is always the
    master executioner."

CHAPTER 75

The people starve because the ruler eats too much
   tax-grain.

Therefore they starve.

They are difficult to rule because their ruler
   does too many things.

Therefore they are difficult to rule.

The people take death lightly because their ruler
   strives for life too vigorously.

Therefore they take death lightly.

It is only those who do not seek after life that
   excel in making life valuable.

   The reason people will avoid him and
   government is disorderly comes from above
   and not from below. People follow those
   above.[1]

NOTE

1. According to Tung Ssu-ching and the
Tao-te chen-ching chi-chu, there are these words
here in the Wang Pi text: [I] suspect that this
[chapter] was not written by Lao Tzu.

CHAPTER 76

When man is born, he is tender and weak.

At death, he is stiff and hard.

All things, the grass as well as trees, are tender
    and supple while alive.

When dead, they are withered and dried.

Therefore the stiff and the hard are companions
    of death.

The tender and the weak are companions of life.

Therefore if the army is strong, it will not win.

    He who strengthens his army to oppress the

    world will be hated by all. Therefore it is

    certain that he will not succeed.

If a tree is stiff, it will break.[1]

    This is brought about by things.

The strong and the great are inferior,

    That means the roots of the tree.

while the tender and the weak are superior.

    That means the branches of the tree.[2]

NOTES

    1. Chan's note (p. 233, note 2): Fu I...,
Yü Yüeh..., and Ma Hsü-lun are unanimous in
saying that ping[a] (soldier) in the Wang Pi text
and kung[b] (together) in the Ho-shang Kung text
are corruptions of the word che[c] (to break).

    2. "Inferior" and "superior" also refer to
the lower or upper portions of the tree.

CHAPTER 77

Heaven's Way is indeed like the bending of a bow.

When (the string) is high, bring it down.

When it is low, raise it up.

When it is excessive, reduce it.

When it is insufficient, supplement it.

The Way of Heaven reduces whatever is excessive
and supplements whatever is insufficient.

The way of man is different.

Only when one's virtue is identical with that
of Heaven and Earth[1] can one embrace all, as
in the case of the Way of Heaven. As in the
case of the capacities of man, each clings to
its own body, and they cannot be equalized.
Only by not clinging to one's own body and not
keeping Nature for oneself can one be identified with the virtue of Heaven and Earth,

It reduces the insufficient to offer to the
excessive.

Who is able to have excess to offer to the world?

Only the man of Tao.

Therefore the sage acts, but does not rely on his
own ability.

He accomplishes his task, but does not claim credit
for it.

He has no desire to display his excellence.

This is to say that Tao alone can be full and
yet completely empty, reduce what it has in

order to make up for what it has not, "soften the light" and "become one with the dusty world,"[2] and be vast and equal. Therefore the sage does not want to display his excellence when making things equal in the world.

NOTES

1. Alluding to the Book of Changes, commentary on hexagram number 1, Ch'ien[a] (Heaven).

2. Quoting Lao Tzu, chapter 4.

CHAPTER 78

There is nothing softer and weaker than water,

And yet there is nothing better for attacking hard
and strong things.

For this reason there is no substitute for it.

I^a (by means of) means to use. Ch'i^b (that
refers to water. It means that there is no
substitute for the use of the softness of water.

All the world knows that the weak overcomes the
strong and the soft overcomes the hard.

But none can practice it.

Therefore the sage says:

He who suffers disgrace for his country

Is called the lord of the land.

He who takes upon himself the country's misfortunes,

Becomes the king of the empire.

Straight words seem to be their opposite.

CHAPTER 79

To patch up great hatred is surely to leave some

hatred behind.

If one has not settled a contract clearly so

that great hatred has resulted, and then

tries to appease by virtue, the injury will not

be healed. Therefore there remains some

hatred.

How can this be regarded as good?

Therefore the sage keeps the left-hand portion

(obligation) of a contract[1]

The left-hand portion of a contract is to

prevent the cause of hatred.

And does not blame the other party.

Virtuous people attend to their left-hand portions,

Virtuous people are mindful of their contract

and do not allow hatred to arise and then

blame others.

While those without virtue attend to other people's

mistakes.

Other people's mistakes mean attending to

people's errors.

"The Way of Heaven has no favorite.

It is always with the good man."[2]

NOTES

1. Chan's note (p. 237, note 1): In ancient times, contracts were written on two bamboo slips which fitted together. The left one, being a symbol of inferiority, was given the debtor.

2. Chan's note (p. 237, note 2): These sayings, probably an ancient proverb, are also found with slight variation in the inscription referred to in chapter 42, note 5.

CHAPTER 80

Let there be a small country with few people.

    A small country with few people can still be
induced to return to former times. How much
more can a big country with many people?
Therefore a small country is mentioned here
for discussion.

Let there be ten times and a hundred times[1] as
    many utensils

But let them not be used.

    This means that although people have ten times
and a hundred times as many utensils but have
no use for them. Why worry about insufficiency?

Let the people value their lives[2] highly and not
    migrate far.

    Let people not use their utensils but only
value their own bodies. Let them not be
greedy for goods and gifts but be contented
with their dwellings. And let them value
their lives highly and not migrate afar.

Even if there are ships and carriages, none will
    ride in them.

Even if there are armor and weapons, none will
    display them.

Let the people again knot cords and use them (in
    place of writing).

Let them relish their food, beautify their
    clothing, be content with their homes, and

delight in their customs.

Though neighboring communities overlook one

another and the crowing of cocks and barking

of dogs can be heard,

Yet the people there may grow old and die without

ever visiting one another.

They will desire nothing.

NOTES

1. Chan's note (p. 238, note 1): According
to Yü Yüeh, shih-po[a] (ten, hundred) means "military
weapons." [Some Japanese commentators] understand
shih-po and ch'i[b] (utensils) to mean "people with
talents ten times or a hundred times more than the
ordinary." In view of the following lines, ch'i
is better understood as "utensils" than as "talents."

2. Chan's note (p. 239, note 2): Literally,
"taking death seriously."

CHAPTER 81

True words are not beautiful;

    Their reality consists of substance.

Beautiful words are not true.

    Their root lies in simplicity.

A good man does not argue;

He who argues is not a good man.

A wise man has no extensive knowledge;

    His ultimate is in the One.

He who has extensive knowledge is not a wise man.

The sage does not accumulate for himself.

    Not selfishly to want things for oneself

    but only to associate with the good. Leave

    things alone, that is all.

The more he uses for others, the more he has

    himself.

    Because people honor him.

The more he gives to others, the more he possesses

    of his own.

    Because people will come to him.

The Way of Heaven is to benefit others and not to

    injure.

    (The Way of Heaven) moves and always produces

    and completes things.

The Way of the sage is to act but not to compete.

    Because the sage follows (the Way of) Heaven

    which only benefits but does not injure.

BIBLIOGRAPHY

Chan, Wing-tsit, "The Evolution of the Neo-Confucian Concept Li as Principle," in Tsing Hua Journal of Chinese Studies, n. s. 4, no. 2 (February, 1964): 123-138; reprinted in Neo-Confucianism, Etc.: Essays by Wing-tsit Chan (Hanover, N.H: Oriental Society, 1969), pp. 45-87

____, A Source Book in Chinese Philosophy (Princeton, N. J.: Princeton University Press, 1963), pp. 314-324

Chao Ping-wen (1159-1232), Tao-te chen-ching chi-chieh (Collected explanations of the True Classic of the Way and Virtue) 趙秉文 道德真經集解

Ch'eng Hsüan-ying (fl. 647-663), Lao Tzu chu (Commentary on the Lao Tzu) 成玄英 老子註

Chiang Hsi-ch'ang, Lao Tzu chiao-ku (Lao Tzu collated and explained) 蔣錫昌 老子校詁

Ch'ien Mu, Chung-kuo ssu-hsiang shih (History of Chinese thought) (Taipei: Chung-hua Wen-hua Ch'u-pen Shih-yeh Wei-yüan-hui, 1952), pp. 88-94 錢穆 中國思想史 中華文化出版事業委員會

____, "Wang Pi Kuo Hsiang chu I Lao Chuang yung li-tzu t'iao-lu" (Cases of the use of the team li in Wang Pi's and Kuo Hsiang's commentaries on the Book of Changes, the Lao Tzu, and the Chuang Tzu), Hsin-Ya hsüeh-pao (New Asia Journal) 1, no. 1 (April, 1955): 137

王弼郭象注易老莊用理字條錄新亞學報

Chou Shao-hsien, <u>Wei-Chin ch'ing-t'an shu-lun</u> (An
account of the Pure Conversation movement of
the Wei and Chin periods, 220-420) (Taipei:
Commercial Press, 1966), pp. 61-70

周紹賢魏晉清談述論

Chou Shih-fu, <u>Chung-kuo che-hsüeh shih</u> (History of
Chinese philosophy) (Taipei: San-min Book Co.,
1972), pp. 214-219 周世輔中國哲學史三民

Den Shiryū, <u>Ō-chū rōshi kokujiben</u> (Wang Pi's
commentary on the <u>Lao Tzu</u> elaborated), 1773

田子龍王注老子國字辯

Fan Shou-k'ang, <u>Wei-Chin chih ch'ing-t'an</u> (The
Pure Conversation movement in the Wei-Chin
period (Shanghai: Commercial Press, 1936),
pp. 16-22 范壽康魏晉之清談

Fu I (555-639), <u>Chiao-ting ku-pen Lao Tzu</u> (Ancient
text of the <u>Lao Tzu</u> collated) 傅奕校定古本老子

Fung Yu-lan, <u>A History of Chinese Philosophy</u>, trans.
by Derk Bodde, Vol. 2 (Princeton, N.J.:
Princeton University Press, 1953), pp. 168-189

____, <u>A Short History of Chinese Philosophy</u> (New
York: Macmillan, 1948), p. 219

____, <u>The Spirit of Chinese Philosophy</u>, trans. by
E. R. Hughes (London: Kegan Paul, 1947), pp.
134-138, 154

Han P'u-hsien, <u>Chung-kuo chung-ku che-hsüeh shih-yao</u>
(Essentials of the history of medieval Chinese

philosophy) (Taipei: Cheng-chung Book Co.,
1960), pp. 72-84
韓逋仙 中國中古哲學史要正中

Hatano Tarō, Lao Tzu Wang chu chiao-cheng (Wang

Pi's commentary on the Lao Tzu collated), Part

I, Journal of Yokohama Municipal University,

Ser. A-1, no. 8 (July, 1952): 1-150; Part II,

ibid., A-3, no. 15 (March, 1953): 1-157; Part

III, ibid., A-8, no. 27 (October, 1954): 1-205
波多野太郎 老子王注校正 横濱市立
大學紀要

Hattori Nankaku (1683-1759), Rōshi dōtokukyō (Lao Tzu,
Classic of the Way and Virtue), quoted in
Hatano 服部南郭 老子道德經

Ho Ch'ang-ch'ün, Wei-Chin ch'ing-t'an ssu-hsiang

ch'u-lun (Preliminary discussion on the thoughts

of the Pure Conversation movement of the Wei-

Chin period) (Shanghai: Commercial Press,

1946), pp. 43-45, 63-81
賀昌群 魏晉清談思想初論

Ho Ch'i-ming, Wei-Chin ssu-hsiang yü t'an-feng

(Thought and conversational style of the Wei-

Chin period) (Taipei: Commercial Press, 1967),

pp. 74-102 何啟民 魏晉思想與談風

Ho-shang Kung (fl. 179-159 B.C.?), Lao Tzu chu

(Commentary on the Lao Tzu) 河上公老子註

Hou Wai-lu, Chung-kuo ssu-hsiang t'ung-shih (General

history of Chinese thought), vol. 3 (Peking:

214

Jen-min Ch'u-pen-she, 1957), pp. 95-96, 110-122

侯外廬 中國思想通史 人民出版社

"Hsiang-erh". See Lao Tzu.

I Shun-ting (1858-1920), Tu Lao cha-chi (Notes from
reading the Lao Tzu) 易順鼎 讀老札記

Jao Tsung-i, Lao Tzu hsiang-erh chu chiao-chien (The
"hsiang-erh" commentary on the Lao Tzu collated
and commented on) (Hong Kong: 1956)

饒宗頤 老子想爾註校箋

Jen Chi-yü, Chung-kuo che-hsüeh shih chien-pien
(Brief history of Chinese philosophy) (Peking:
Jen-min Ch'u-pen-she, 1974), pp. 251-262

任繼愈 中國哲學史簡編

Jung Chao-tsu, Wei-Chin te tzu-jan chu-i (Naturalism
in the Wei-Chin period) (Shanghai: Commercial
Press, 1935), pp. 1-9, 14-30

容肇祖 魏晉的自然主義

Kanō Naoki (1868-1947), Chūgoku tetsugaku shi
(History of Chinese philosophy) (Tokyo: Iwanami
Shoten, 1953), pp. 309-313

狩野直喜 中國哲學史 岩波書店

Kao Heng, Ch'ung-ting Lao Tzu cheng-ku (Revised
collation of the Lao Tzu) (Peking: Ku-chi Ch'u-
pen-she, 1956) 高亨重訂老子正詁 古籍出版社

Kuo Chan-po, Chung-kuo chung-ku ssu-hsiang shih
(History of medieval Chinese thought) (Hong
Kong: Lungmen Book Co., 1967), pp. 234-240

郭湛波 中國中古思想史 龍門

Lao Ssu-kwang, Chung-kuo che-hsüeh shih (History
of Chinese philosophy) vol. 2 (Hong Kong:
Chung Chi College, 1971), pp. 170-177
勞思光 中國哲學史崇基

Lao Tzu, The Way of Lao Tzu, trans. by Wing-tsit
Chan (Indianapolis, Indiana: Bobbs-Merrill
Co., 1963)

Lao Tzu hsiang-erh chu (Hsiang-erh commentary of the
Lao Tzu) 老子想爾註

Liu Kuo-chün, "Lao Tzu Wang chu chiao-chi" (Notes
on the collation of Wang Pi's commentary on the
Lao Tzu) T'u-shu-kuan hsüeh chi-k'an (Library
science quarterly) 8, no. 1 (March, 1934):
91-116 劉國鈞老子王注校記圖書館學
季刊

Lin, Paul J., A Translation of Lao Tzu's Tao Te
Ching and Wang Pi's Commentary (Ann Arbor,
Michigan: Center for Chinese Studies, The
University of Michigan, 1977)

Liu Ta-chieh, Wei-Chin ssu-hsiang lun (On Wei-Chin
thought) (Shanghai: Chung-hua Book Co., 1939),
pp. 90-94 劉大杰魏晉思想論中華

Lu Te-ming (556-627), Ching-tien shih-wen (Explanation of words in the Classics)
陸德明經典釋文

Ma Hsü-lun, Lao Tzu chiao-ku (Lao Tzu collated and
explained) (Peking: Ku-chi Ch'u-pen-she, 1924)
馬叙倫老子校詁老子羣故

216

Ming-huang, Emperor (685-762), Tao-te ching chu

 (Commentary on the Classic of the Way and

 Virtue) 明皇道德經註

Mo Chien-p'u, Chou-i ming-hsiang (Hexagrams of the

 Book of Changes explained) (Hong Kong: Tun-mei

 College, 1962), pp. 1-34 莫儉溥周易明象敦梅

Mou Tsung-san, Ts'ai-hsing yü hsüan-li (Capacity,

 nature, and metaphysics) (Hong Kong: Jen-sheng

 Ch'u-pen-she, 1962), pp. 100-167

 牟宗三才性與玄理 人生出版社

____, Wei-Chin hsüan-hsüeh (Wei-Chin metaphysics)

 (Taichung: Tung Hai College, 1962), pp. 37-73

 魏晉玄學 東海

Pi Yüan (1730-1798), Lao Tzu tao-te ching k'ao-i

 (Inquiry into the variants in the Lao Tzu, the

 Classic of the Way and Virtue), Hsün-ching T'ang

 series 畢沅老子道德經攷異訓經堂

Shimada Kan (1879-1915), Ku-wen chiu-shu k'ao

 (Inquiry on old works in the ancient script),

 quoted in Hatano 島田翰古文舊書攷

Tao-te chen-ching chi-chu (Collected commentaries on

 the True Classic of the Way and Virtue)

 道德真經集註

Takeuchi Yoshiō (1879-1915), Rōshi gen shi (Origins

 of the Lao Tzu) (Tokyo: Shimizu-Kōbundō, 1967)

 pp. 62-66 武內義雄老子原始清水弘文堂

____, Rōshi no kenkyū (Study of the Lao Tzu) 3rd

 ed. (Tokyo: Kaizosha, 1947), pp. 123-125

 老子の研究 改造社

T'ang Yung-t'ung, "Wang Pi's New Interpretation of the I-ching and Lun-yu", trans. by Walter Liebenthal, Harvard Journal of Asiatic Studies 9 (1947): 124-161 湯用彤

_____, Wei-Chin hsüan-hsüeh lun-kao (Draft treatise on Wei-Chin metaphysics) (Peking: Jen-min Ch'u-pen-she, 1957), pp. 62-102 魏晉玄學論稿

_____ and Jen Chi-yü, Wei-Chin hsüan-hsüeh chung te she-hui cheng-chih ssu-hsiang lüeh-lun (Brief discussion on social and political thought in Wei-Chin metaphysics) (Shanghai: Jen-min Ch'u-pen-she, n. d.), pp. 21-26 任繼愈 魏晉玄學中的社會政治思想略論

T'ao Hung-ch'ing (1860-1918), Tu chu-tzu cha-chi (Notes on reading the various philosophers) (Shanghai: Chung Hua Book Co., 1919), chapter 1 陶鴻慶 讀諸子札記

Tōjō Ichitō (Hiroshi, 1778-1857), Rōshi ō-chū hyō-shiki (Points noted on Wang Pi's commentary on the Lao Tzu), 1814 東條一堂弘老子王注標識

Tsukada Taihō (1745-1832), Tsuka-chū rōshi kōhon (Draft of Tsukada's commentary on the Lao Tzu), 1804 冢田大峰冢註老子稿本

Tung Ssu-ching (of the Sung Dynasty, 960-1279), Tao-te ching chi-chieh (Collected explanations of the Classic of the Way and Virtue) 董思靖道德經集解

Usami Shinsui (Meguni, 1710-1776), Ō-chū rōshi dōtoku kyō (Wang Pi's commentary on the Lao Tzu), 宇佐美灊水惠、王注老子道德經

218

1769

Wang Chung-min, Lao Tzu k'ao (Inquiry on the Lao
Tzu) (Peking: Chung-hua T'u-shu-kuan Hsieh-
hui, 1927) 王重民 老子考 中華圖書館協會

Wang Pi (226-249), Chou-i lüeh-li (Simple exemplification of the principles of the Book of
Changes), Han-Wei ts'ung-shu (Collection of
works of the Han [B.C. 206-220 A.D.] and Wei
Dynasties) 王弼 周易略例 漢魏叢書

Wright, Arthur F., review of A. A. Petrov, Wang Pi
(224-249): His Place in the History of Chinese
Philosophy, in Harvard Journal of Asiatic
Studies 10 (1947): 75-88

Wu Ch'eng (1249-1333), Tao-te ching chu (Commentary
on the Classic of the Way and Virtue)
吳澄 道德經註

Yang Jung-kuo, Chien-ming Chung-kuo che-hsüeh shih
(Simple history of Chinese philosophy) (Peking:
Jen-min Ch'u-pen-she, 1973), pp. 118-122
楊榮國 簡明中國哲學史

Yen Ling-feng, Chung-wai Lao Tzu chu-shu mu-lu
(Bibliography on the Lao Tzu in Chinese and
foreign languages) (Taipei: Chung-hua Ts'ung-
shu Wei-yüan-hui, 1957) 嚴靈峯 中外老子
著述目錄 中華叢書委員會

_____, T'ao Hung-ch'ing Lao Tzu Wang Pi chu k'an-wu
pu-cheng (Corrections on T'ao Hung-ch'ing's
"Wang Pi's Commentary on the Lao Tzu Corrected")

(Taipei: Wu-ch'iu-pei Chai, 1957) 閻鴻麐
老子王弼注勘誤補正無求備齋

Yu Ying-shih, "Han Chin chih-chi shih chih hsin-tzu-
    chüeh yü hsin-ssu-ch'ao" (New self-awareness
    and new thought of intellectuals in the third
    century), Hsin-Ya hsüeh-pao 4, no. 1 (August
    1959): 88-93, 104-106 余英時魏晉之
際士之新自覺與新思潮

Yü Yüeh (1821-1906), Chu-tzu p'ing-li (Textual
    critique of the various philosophers), 1936
    ed. 愈樾 諸子平議

Zia, N. Z., "Hsien-ts'un Tao-te ching chu-shih shu-
    mu k'ao-lüeh" (Brief inquiry on annotations and
    commentaries on the Classic of the Way and
    Virtue), Nan-hua Shioa-chu Shan-fang wen-chi
    (Collected works of the Nan-hua Hsiao-chu Shan-
    fang) (Hong Kong: South Sky Book Co., 1971)
謝扶雅 現存道德經注釋書目考畧
南華小住山房文集

a	老子		aa	末
b	王弼		ab	德
c	自然		ac	因
d	神器		ad	任
e	無有		ae	順
f	有		af	性
g	道		ag	輔　嗣平陽凱絮卅表
h	理		ah	高　山
i	體　用		ai	山
j	常		aj	王　凱
k	墨　子		ak	王　荊
l	荀　子		al	荊　表
m	莊　非子		am	劉　業
n	韓　子		an	業　玄
o	魏		ao	玄
p	郭　象		ap	蔡　邕徽
q	銳　樣		aq	裴
r	通　理		ar	魏
s	本　理		as	何　晏始黎爽融李湛子
t	出　然之理		at	正
u	研　以然之理		au	王
v	至　理		av	曹
w	程　頤		aw	荀
x	本　體用		ax	趙
y	湯　形		ay	張　子
z	本		az	列

ba 四部備要

bb 聚珍

bc 武英

bd 飛 說之經

be 道德經

bf 熊克

bg 經典釋文

bh 陸德明

bi 老子道德經

bj 隋書

bk 玄言新記道德

bl 舊唐書

bm 新唐書注

bn 老子注

bo 老宗史

bp 武內

bq 萬曆

br 張之象

bs 永樂大典

bt 陶慶鴻

bu 劉國鈞

bv 波靈書

bw 嚴野峯

bx 漢爾陵

by 想張

bz 張陵

ca 河公

cb 高誘

cc 玄

cd 淮南子

ce 牟子玄

cf 舊玄

cg 馬叙倫

ch 四庫全書總目提要

ci 道經

cj 德經

ck 王重民

cl 王卷

cm 道藏

cn 老子微旨畧例

co 何劭

cp 道畧論

cq 老子畧論

cr 老子旨例畧

cs 老子旨畧

ct 道德畧歸

cu 謝扶雅

cv 牟宗三

cw 墨

cx 墨陳榮捷

cy 墨翟

cz 四部叢刊

da 蜀卿周

db 莊清華

dc 清華

dd 王弼郭象注易老並用理字條録

Chapter 1

b 是
c 寞
d 至

Chapter 13

a 驚
b 寵

Chapter 14

a 名
b 何
c 程　頤
d 易　傳
e 治
f 始

Chapter 15

a 理　趣
b 德　趣
c 意
d 容
e 客
f 藏
g 敕

Chapter 16

a 分
b 知
c 真
d 生
e 王

f 周
g 乾
h 極
i 窮　極

Chapter 17

a 太　上
b 不
c 下
d 法

Chapter 18

a 道
b 進

Chapter 19

a 文
b 傑
c 善

Chapter 20

a 夾
b 明
c 名

Chapter 21

a 孔
b 嘆
c 貌
d 說
e 闕

Chapter 23

a 美

b 以無為為君

c 以無為為居

d 體

e 得

f 德

Chapter 24

a 卻 至

b 晉

c 左 傳

d 左 丘 明

e 成

Chapter 25

a 始

b 殆

c 孝經

Chapter 27

a 資

b 襲

c 習

d 齊

e 濟

Chapter 28

a 器

Chapter 29

a 器

b 至

c 性

d 情

Chapter 30

a 始

b 治

c 者

d 有

Chapter 31

a 敦煌

Chapter 32

a 樸散

Chapter 33

a 改

b 攻

Chapter 34

a 力

Chapter 35

a 不 爽

Chapter 36

a 利

Chapter 37

a 治

b 始

Chapter 38

a 德

b 得

c 禮

d 復

e 至

f 志

g 直
h 真
i 捨
j 居
k 陽
l 暢
m 失 禮/豊
n 夫 禮
o 前
p 誠
q 僞

Chapter 39
a 至
b 致
c 譽
d 輿

Chapter 41
a 宮
b 商

Chapter 42
a 氣
b 說 苑
c 劉 向
d 必
e 非

Chapter 43
a 出 於

Chapter 45
a 冲
b 充
c 一
d 已

Chapter 47
a 名
b 明

Chapter 50
a 韓非子

Chapter 51
a 德
b 失
c 尊

Chapter 52
a 功

Chapter 53
a 介 然
b 施
c 爲

Chapter 55
a 全
b 祥
c 昭

Chapter 57
a 已
b 民

Chapter 58

a 廉

Chapter 62

a 奧

b 市尊行

c 里

Chapter 63

a 居

b 邑

Chapter 64

a 里

Chapter 67

a 不肖

b 慈

c 陳

d 陣

Chapter 73

a 誰

b 齊

c 濟

Chapter 76

a 兵

b 共

c 折

Chapter 77

a 乾

Chapter 78

a 以人

b 其

Chapter 80

a 什伯

b 器

Dr. Ariane Rump resides in Zurich, Switzerland. After translating the Lao Tzu, she became interested in Wang Pi, the third-century metaphysician. Her research efforts were supported by a scholarship from from the Board of Education and the University of Zurich

Professor Wing-tsit Chan is Anna R. D. Gillespie Professor of Philosophy at Chatham College, Pittsburgh, Pennsylvania. He is the leading authority in Chinese philosophy and the author of numerous journal articles and books, including A Source Book in Chinese Philosophy.

SOCIETY FOR ASIAN AND COMPARATIVE PHILOSOPHY

MONOGRAPH SERIES

No. 1   Ronald G. Dimberg   The Sage and Society:
The Life and Thought of Ho Hsin-yin $4.75

No. 2   Eliot Deutsch Studies in Comparative
Aesthetics $3.50

No. 3   Wei-ming Tu Centrality and Commonality:
An Essay on Chung-yung $5.00

No. 4   Gottfried Wilhelm Leibniz, Discourse on the
Natural Theology of the Chinese, translated
with commentaries by Henry Rosemont, Jr. and
Daniel J. Cook $5.00

No. 5   Kisor K. Chakrabarti   The Logic of Gotama
                                         $4.00

No. 6   Wang Pi Commentary on the Lao Tzu,
translated by Ariane Rump in collaboration
with Wing-tsit Chan $

Orders for SACP monographs should be directed to
The University Press of Hawaii, 2840 Kolowalu Street,
Honolulu, Hawaii 96822 USA. Remittance in US
funds should accompany order.

2337